A YEAR *in the* COMPANY *of* ANGELS

A Pilgrim on Spruce Island

ANTHONY LINDERMAN

ANCIENT FAITH PUBLISHING

CHESTERTON, INDIANA

Published by:
Ancient Faith Publishing
A Division of Ancient Faith Ministries
1050 Broadway, Suite 6
Chesterton, IN 46304

Unless otherwise noted, Scripture quotations are taken from the New King James Version, © 1979, 1980, 1982 by Thomas Nelson, Inc. Used by permission.

Cover art & design: Amber Schley Iragui; angel illustrations: Sophie Ries

ISBN: 978-1-955890-91-5

Library of Congress Control Number: 2025946992

For the Fathers and Brothers of St. Michael's Skete

CONTENTS

MICHAEL

Especially the shy, especially the brave,
Especially the coats of dew
Worn by the soldier and the slave,
Especially the happy songs
Of maybright girls at play,
These, and these especially,
St. Michael longs to save.
When paschal stones and paschal flames
Fall out of lilac heaven and the Song
Somehow, spagyrically, makes shadows start to smoke
Like sweet incense, when all the fear of night
Is filled with stronger presences,
And the seductive moon
Is worn like as an Aegis
Upon the arm of our enhallowed Mars,
Our Michael, and our Who is Like the Lord
Surrounds the question and the ache:
He rolls away the stone as dawn begins to break.

—J. Z. Schafer[1]

---

1   Used with permission.

GABRIEL

So Gabriel
Walked on the water and the ancient tears
Of those expelled from Paradise
Fell down through greying air upon his wings;
But on the water's face were lilies strewn,
When Gabriel first in newest worlds drew breath,
Returning like as Hermes to the throne of Zeus
With beautiful responses to relay,
Words born as mixture of the lightning and the dew,
Because the Hebrew girl had said,
"Amen amen, I am the handmaid of the Lord."
And in these words did Paradise,
Reclining like a lion, stretch His legs.

—J. Z. Schafer[2]

---

2   Used with permission.

FOREWORD

Dear Reader,

There are places in this world . . . and then there are places. All of Alaska lies firmly in the second camp, and in particular the sister islands of Kodiak, Spruce, and St. Nilus, which are located not far from the base of the Aleutian chain. To set foot on them, imbued as they are with wild beauty and awesome power and the grace of abundant life, is to enter not only a new world but a new mind, a new way of being.

If you've not yet been, and if you know nothing of St. Herman of Alaska, I challenge you to spend two weeks within the enchanting yet forbidding land and seascape which that kind and holy man made his own between the years 1794 and 1837. By the end of your stay, you will have discovered for yourself three spiritual realities: that Alaska, somehow, has become a kind of additional Christian Holy Land; that St. Herman is its guardian; and that St. Herman was so close in spirit to his co-novice at the monastery of Sarov, that he and St. Seraphim might fairly be thought of as fraternal twins in their paths to Christ.

It may be that no one you meet there happens to state these facts right out loud, but as I say, you will still see them for yourself.

As I write this foreword in 2025, it seems possible that Orthodoxy in the United States may have found a new home here in our land. Perhaps we should have seen earlier that there is too much love in the American heart for wild nature, for immediate participation in the life of the Bible, and for honest personal freedom, for Orthodox Christianity *not* to have become almost inevitable for so many of us. Moreover, for Americans, our roots in the islands west of continental Europe convey to us naturally those places' own historic affinity for Byzantine spirituality. And if it continues to be the case that so many Americans find in Orthodoxy a mirror showing them their own truest selves in Christ, then perhaps Alaska, and her many islands in particular, will become for us a kind of new Mount Athos, summoning American men *and* American women to the life of hesychastic daring that their spiritual ancestors among the Celts of the British Isles so beautifully pursued.

I don't want to say much more than that in this short foreword, for I feel that I shouldn't delay your departure any further. The ocean tide is shifting, and it's already time for you to step into the trusty skiff *Archangel* and head out for yourself. Your brilliant captain in these pages, although not so very long ago my student at seminary, is also a young man I have admired since the moment I met him, as well as an authentic poet-theologian. You may feel the little boat tipping at times, but have no fear. The *Archangel* knows the waves and will not allow him or you to sink. And I am confident that your grace-filled journey with this captain will furnish you with bright memories and bring to mind both tears and laughter for many days to come.

The boat is leaving now! I wish you luck!

When you get there, would you please pray for me, too?

And may our crucified and risen Savior, the Lord Jesus Christ, be with you, and with everyone.

Sincerely,
Timothy Patitsas
Assistant Professor of Christian Ethics
Holy Cross Greek Orthodox School of Theology
Author, *The Ethics of Beauty*

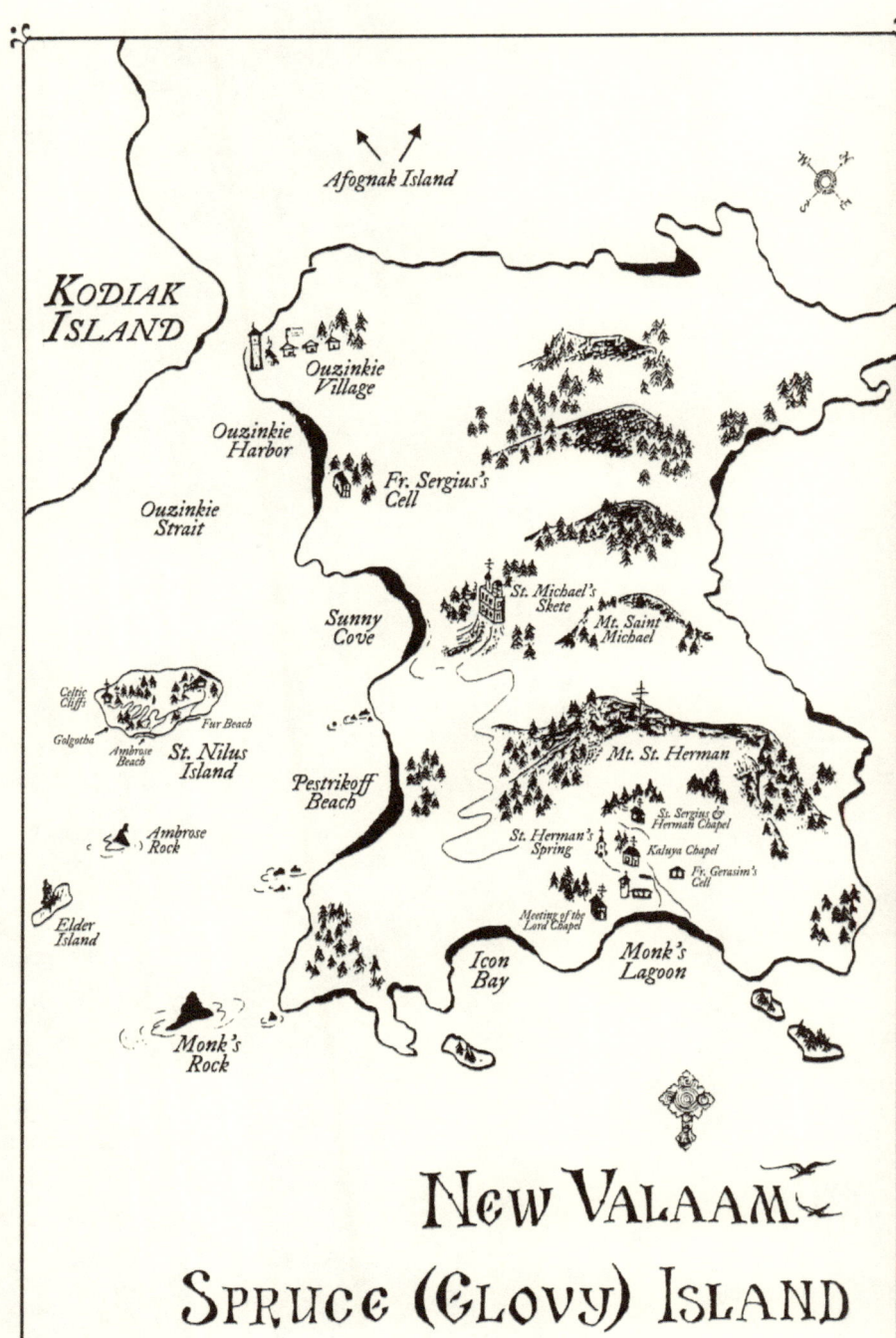

Afognak Island

KODIAK
ISLAND

Ouzinkie
Village

Ouzinkie
Harbor

Ouzinkie
Strait

Fr. Sergius's
Cell

Sunny
Cove

St. Michael's
Skete

Mt. Saint
Michael

Celtic
Cliffs

Fur Beach

Golgotha

Ambrose
Beach

St. Nilus
Island

Pestrikoff
Beach

Mt. St. Herman

St. Sergius &
Herman Chapel

St. Herman's
Spring

Kaluya Chapel

Fr. Gerasim's
Cell

Ambrose
Rock

Meeting of the
Lord Chapel

Elder
Island

Icon
Bay

Monk's
Lagoon

Monk's
Rock

NEW VALAAM

SPRUCE (ELOVY) ISLAND

Mount
St. Herman
Cross

Ss. Sergius &
Herman of Valaam
Chapel

St. Herman's
Spring

Kaluga
Chapel

Fr. Gerasim's
Cell

Meeting of the Lord Chapel

Monk's Creek

M O N K ' S   L A G O O N

Introduction

THE LITTLE ENTRANCE
OF THE SILVER SALMON

S UNNY COVE BEACH IS THE narthex of Spruce Island, a threshold of stone, sand, and water. During the long summer days I walked down to the western bluff of the cove where an old, abandoned house sits overlooking the gleaming water in the low Alaskan sun. On a calm day the surface takes on the appearance of a great aqueous pane of stained glass with huge sapphire and emerald abysses, as if reflecting jewels from the Lord's throne in the heavens. On other days, like that of my arrival, the heavy curtains of the clouds are thrown across the windows of the sky as if to direct one's attention downward to find God's hidden throne in the depths of His creation. Such was my first passage from Kodiak Island to Spruce Island, over water, amid a cloud of mist.

The mist hid the horizon; it crowded the borders of my vision until the visible world shrank to the side of the monk's small skiff as it eased its way across the unseen waves of the channel. The rolling deck was almost a membrane under my feet, an aluminum suspension scarcely more solid than the water tension through which it cut. When we hit a wave hard, the spray leapt at me like a savage caress, causing me to all but laugh at the sea's insistence of its there-ness, its assurance that I passed only with its blessing. These were forces I had only read about, and now their reality arrested my attention with such potency that the world, over which I had trudged for so far and so long, regained the strangeness it once had during the summer I was five years old.

One afternoon, my family and I had just gone on a hayride, followed by s'mores at the farmhouse. Looking out over the fields that evening in the sunset, a wordless joy thrilled me that I lived in a world of hayrides, s'mores, and endless wonders. Decades later, Fr. Andrew, who piloted the boat, standing to the right of the tiller with my weight balancing the vessel to his left, would soon include in a sermon Dostoyevsky's quote, "One good memory from childhood can save us." One vision from Eden from a time before we ate from the tree can smolder in the depths of the soul until the winds of the Gulf of Alaska fan it to life once more.

Because creation fell with Adam, it too needs a garment to keep it from the withering gaze of his cynicism. Now at last the mist came draping across the horizon like a cosmic curtain. The mist was the partition, stretching from the sea to the sky, of a hidden chamber of reality from which I had been exiled for so long.

Oh, the years of hearing rumors, second- and thirdhand. How I had longed to stray in an enchanted wood, to pass through a wardrobe, to encounter a book spacious enough for all of me, not just my imagination. And, just when I had given up searching, I found myself traveling there in the body. Clock time foundered as the mist covered my inner sundial. I grinned as I held on. This was better than reading because I was at last in a book, the big book that St. Maximos called the Fifth Gospel of Nature. I had stepped inside the Psalter. That night at the vigil for St. John Maximovich I would hear:

This great and wide sea,
In which are innumerable teeming things,
Living things both small and great.

There the ships sail about;
There is that Leviathan
Which You have made to play there. (Ps. 104:25–26)

There I was, Psalm 104-ing on a ship sailing about. I was a teeming, living thing, both small and great. Another day Fr. Andrew would throttle down, and we would see the humpback whales cresting and blowing beside our boat—Leviathan sporting about.

It felt as if I had been moving through the world with the greatest effort of self-propulsion, compared to this quickening. It was as if I had fallen into a crease of the world, a ley line of reality—as if the skiff were an aluminum splinter caught in the same electromagnetic field by which the salmon navigate to the place of their birth on the ridges of the ocean floor. Now a subterranean lodestone drew us into the liturgy of the sea. I was an altar boy in the Little Entrance of the Silver Salmon.

Liturgical historians teach us that the Little Entrance was once the entry of the faithful into the church from a separate building. There is an echo of this procession also in entrance of the bishop into the sanctuary from the narthex during Orthros. Nature, being the Fifth Gospel, further echoed this procession by leading Fr. Andrew and me to the narthex of Spruce Island. I hopped off the last rung of the boat's ladder to the threshold of the island, feeling the stones of the beach under my soles and the cool of the water. I stood in that space that was not quite water and not quite stone, just as a narthex is church but not quite sanctuary. In many ancient churches the angels are depicted there watching, ushering you into the nave. Likewise, gesturing deeper into the island with her prow was the monks' skiff I had just ridden in—*Archangel*.

At that time, I knew no knots to tie her off. So Fr. Andrew fixed her to the running lines but let me pull her out to the buoy so she would not go dry. Next, he took my bag and bungeed it to the four-wheeler. He explained that he would ride ahead but pause at every fork in the path to St. Michael's Skete and show me which turn to take. Little did I know how well I would come to learn every bend of that path. Little did I know how many times I would follow that priest up the hill. On misty days the colors have a paradoxical, dun vividness. Unbleached by the sun, the mosses, spruce needles, and leafy bushes seem to glow with their own native luminosity. The sun, still sustaining them, steps off the stage of the day to let the widest array of greens I have ever seen present themselves for the glory of God. Most people imagined the frozen Yukon when I told them I was living in Alaska, but the Kodiak Archipelago is in far southern Alaska. Here the climate allows for a temperate rainforest, with all the lushness that word implies. Through that world of green, the red fender of the four-wheeler beckoned brightly with Fr. Andrew looking encouragingly over his shoulder just to throttle further up and further in.

The highest structure on the hill of Sunny Cove is St. Michael's Skete. Its walls are firehouse red, and its windows are all different sizes, contemplating the channel and Mt. Monashka. I couldn't see that view in the mist, but on my third day the sky cleared so that from the high windows of the skete every level of the cosmos was revealed—from the distant blows of the humpbacks on the water to the eagles soaring high against the mountain heights. The first day, when I arrived huffing to the top of the hill, everything was still hidden, and all the intimations of the grandeur of the cosmos were concentrated in the refectory through the lower-level door. Father Andrew showed me the bootjack to peel off my muddy Xtratufs. I stepped unshod into the honey-colored coziness of the dining hall, where the spruce boards were long seasoned by the scent of many meals, the merry crackle of the woodstove, and the incense wafting down from the chapel upstairs. I entered in my socks.

That summer of 2022, I was in dire need of spiritual renewal. I was wrung out after finishing the academic year as an eleventh-grade English Language Arts teacher. Quite at random I ran into a friend who suggested I make a pilgrimage to Spruce Island, Alaska—the island on which the Russian missionary St. Herman lived his holy life, sanctifying the land for all time. It hadn't even been on my radar. I had been thinking that I would make a trip to Greece, as I had during my time at Holy Cross Greek Orthodox School of Theology, but the unknown had an immediate appeal to me.

My point of contact for Spruce Island was my beloved friend, professor, and mentor, Dr. Timothy Patitsas. In his ethics class he had taught us that God's theophany, His appearing to the world, is beautiful in a way that everyone can understand. But it is also "beauty-for-us," a personal theophany hidden within a general appearance-making, in which God makes Himself known to each person in a specific way. God reveals Himself to each of us through a beauty that strikes us as deliberate—as a gift that only God could have known us well enough to give.

From the first glimpse of the skiff materializing through the mist, my stay at the skete was shot through with such gifts. For example, when I arrived there, I discovered that the three most important icons of the Mother of God in my life were all present on the walls of the second floor just downstairs from my cell.

The cell that I ultimately stayed in is called the Tower, a single-room turret—a crow's nest popping out of the east side of the building. The room had a window looking out to the water, and beneath the window sat a desk on which the first essays in this book were written. Immediately down the Tower's ladder is the vestry of the little Chapel of St. Michael. In that small room is a closet for vestments and a shelf containing carefully ordered icons of the saints who are celebrated each day of the year. In the corner is a confession stand that holds the Gospel and a cross. A bureau contains many small gifts and holy oils, and above it, under the ladder, is a life-sized copy of Panagia of Jerusalem, an icon I had venerated in the Holy Land with Dr. Patitsas on our senior pilgrimage from Holy Cross. Saint Paisios, who was deemed worthy to see the Mother of God, once said this icon captured her likeness the most.

The vestry has an open door to the altar, and on the other side of the holy table on a corner shelf is the icon of the Theotokos of the Inexhaustible Cup of Serpukhov. I had stood before this very icon multiple times and said its akathist with a dear brother. To the immediate left of the hallway door is a huge copy of the miracle-working icon Panagia Kexaritomeni, from the Xenophontos Monastery on Mount Athos. When I had visited there, I wanted to venerate the original, and the fathers brought it out from the altar to me. In it our Most Holy Lady is wearing a richly embroidered mantle and gestures to her Son, who squirms in her arms, tilting His head at an angle as He looks at the viewer.

These encounters are what I mean by general and personal theophany: Anyone might be struck by the radiant beauty of these icons. However, to me the fact that all three were present carried the shocking force of revelation. The personal time and space of my life seemed concentrated together on the second floor of the skete. The icons of my previous pilgrimage were gathered within arm's reach of each other. The liturgical seasons of the year were contained in the colors of the vestments in the closet. The saints of each day were all present in icons on a single wall of the vestry, and every morning I climbed down the ladder into their company.

When I lay sick on my bed, the Liturgy continued on the floor below—Fr. Andrew vesting for the services, the incense wafting up the tower to soothe, purge, and align the sickness of my soul and body. I, who loved the ivory tower of academia, the lofty heights of the rational mind, was housed in a physical tower so that, reunited, body and mind might be wooed together by Beauty. I was called down from regions of the air to rejoin the Divine Liturgy of St. John Chrysostom taking place on the second floor, the middle floor of the cosmos—what the Norse called Midgard or the "Middle Enclosure." This was not the subterranean liturgy of salmon, nor was it a disembodied airiness of the mind. Before the altar the priest stands as mediator at the divide of the horizon, made of earth but with lungs full of sky. Every morning at 3 a.m. I stumbled down from dreams to the reality of Matins. My tiredness or disorientation were no matter as I passed into a perfectly oriented space beneath the wakeful eyes of the saints, with the iconographic stars painted on the ceiling of the chapel mirroring the glistening firmament overhead.

With the permission of my spiritual father and the hegumen of the monastery, Fr. Andrew, I extended my stay in Alaska through July. Amazingly, the month-long stay did not make the striking beauty more prosaic. It just meant that, against all odds, I was being allowed to remain in Paradise. The grand rubric of creation was durable and could not be ruined by someone who had not learned his place in it.

As the month progressed and the specter of the next school year loomed large, I realized that I did not want to go back to Boston. Of course, no one wants an otherworldly pilgrimage to end, but for me, the thought of leaving after experiencing a theophany—one God had clearly woven together just for me—inspired a special dread. How I have loved the moment in *The Hobbit* when Gandalf appears, looking for someone "to share in an adventure." How often had my heart thrilled as a boy, wishing for that call—with a boy's certainty that I would answer it without hesitating. Something went wrong, though; I pressed my hand into the wardrobe and did not find Narnia. Now, was it too late? Had I grown too old? Chesterton writes at the end of *Orthodoxy*, "It may be that He has the eternal appetite of infancy; for we have sinned and grown old, and our Father is younger than we."[3]

In 2022 I was 28, but inside I felt arthritic and bent double. I had not broached the subject of staying longer with Fr. Andrew. I feared he would kindly, but firmly, say no—especially because I did not necessarily feel a call to a monastic vocation. I just wanted to stay in Eden for a while. However, while we were on a mail run, outside the post office he said, "You know—and there is absolutely no pressure here—but you would be most welcome to stay with us, if that is what you wanted."

I still cannot think of it without being moved. Here I had been preparing a proposal in my head, ready even to offer a stipend from my savings for room and board since I was not formally going to be a pre-novice. Instead, he anticipated my request. I wrote to him later that his offer reminded me of a line from the Mumford and Sons song, "Not With Haste": "And I was broke, I was on my knees / but you said 'Yes,' as I said 'Please.'"

I called the principal of the high school, telling him of my resignation before I sent out the letter. He was most gracious, and just like that, I could stay. I was composed when I called Mom about the decision, but that same evening I left chapel to cry in the corridor in front of Panagia Kexaritomeni. This was new territory. It was the first decision I had ever made that felt inspired not by necessity, but by Beauty. And Beauty, as I hope to convey in the following stories, is marked by its mildness. It never forces, manipulates, or withholds.

---

3   G. K. Chesterton, *Orthodoxy* (John Lane Company, 1909), 107.

It woos.

The next ten and a half months at the monastery, I began a strange courtship with the Beautiful. I tagged along in the procession of the salmon. I romped up the Sunny Cove hill behind Fr. Andrew's bike. I came down from my Tower each morning and raced my fellow pilgrims to the beach to where the *Archangel* with her merry bob waited expectantly on the running lines. As with all great romance, precious little can be spoken of without betrayal. The following essays are just a few stitches of the train of the robe woven by the music of what happens in this world.

1

ᴇNTER THE CASTLE

"N O ONE SETS FOOT ON Mount Athos without the blessing of the Mother of God," said Dr. Timothy Patitsas while we were on pilgrimage together. I believed him. Even the visible gatekeepers did not seem surmountable without help: those middle-aged Greek men peering down at my documents, looking both imperial and bored in the Mount Athos passport office. They were the inheritors of the mythological Charon who ferried the dead across the river Styx, to say nothing of the unseen guardian who keeps the gates of Eden with a naked sword of flame.

So, I was a nervous pilgrim among nervous pilgrims at the passport office, hoping that the fathers of Xenophontos Monastery had notified these professional Frowners at Documents of my permission to visit. At last, when my pass was printed in an archaic font, with the length of my stay and a lovely stamp at the top, I was much relieved. The pass worked like the silver coin placed under the tongue of the dead, the price of a soul's passage, paid to Charon—or in this case, Charalambos, the clean-shaven ferryman who waved me aboard with barely a glance.

After this the sight of *any* monastery from the sunlit deck of the boat would have thrilled me. I felt I was in on the secret now, and Panagia was allowing me to step ashore on her mountain. This doesn't happen to just anyone. Half of humankind are women, who are not allowed to come here, and most of the other half doesn't know to come here. So when at last Xenophontos Monastery came into view, I was delighted to find it was a glorious, millennium-old Byzantine castle: tall, with gated walls encircling a tiny city, out of whose center rises a church with striking red-tile domes.

Absolutely everyone has a hidden desire to live in a castle, a desire that pops up in the strangest of places. Taking Shotokan karate classes as a kid, I struggled to remember the sequence of moves that comprised the third kata. The best student, a seventeen-year-old brown belt, was beyond the eight numbered katas. He kicked, leapt, jabbed, and tumbled like a lethal wave through the great kata known as *Bassai Dai,* Enter the Castle. It was a stylized series of attacks and blocks with which a samurai might have won entrance through a press of defenders into an Edo-era fortress: He flew through the kata on the very loosest terms with gravity.

Even my older brother, who sometimes led the exercises, celebrated when he landed a hit on this brown belt. I did not have the honor of sparring with him. Indeed, from the bottom of the class it was all I could do during my bouts to avoid being sat on, for defeat meant being sat on. All of which to say, I never learned Bassai Dai, so I could never have fought my way into a castle. This means that in my travels to the castles of Albania, Spain, and the cliffside mountain keeps of Mount Athos, my entry has always been a gift.

Yet, as unique and wonderful as each had been, holy or less holy, one castle still eluded me. I did not know this consciously, although

I acknowledged a hope that, one day, I might found my own household *à la* "an Englishman's home is his castle." But this wish was just the tip of the iceberg of a longing I did not recognize until my pilgrimage to Spruce Island and St. Michael's Skete.

"No one sets foot on Spruce Island without the blessing of St. Herman," Dr. Patitsas insisted again this year when I told him my destination. There, off remote Kodiak Island, Spruce's guardians are the tempestuous waves of the Gulf of Alaska. Sometimes the weather is so inclement that a skiff cannot make harbor or safely depart the island for weeks at a time. Yet through the grace of St. Herman, I arrived in Kodiak to find that the fog-covered water was calm. There was no ferry, just the monks' skiff, the *Archangel.*

She's a lady, with a prow that almost lifts to flight as she crests the waves; the touch of the helmsman is so light, so sure, that it seems that at any moment the little craft will take wing, and no one will be surprised to see the *Archangel* fly. The hands at the till are those of the hegumen of St. Michael's Skete, Fr. Andrew Wermouth, who has come to Kodiak in the *Archangel* to pick me up. No passport, ticket, or silver coin needed.

I was received with warm monastic hospitality, and the skete guesthouse, built at the base of a huge pine, is welcoming in the midsummer twilight. The air is fragrant with spruce, and the moss beneath my feet soft enough to sleep on. The whole island seems untouched, waiting to be explored.

Later, I received a blessing to stay by myself for two nights at the skete's cabin at Monk's Lagoon, on the eastern shore of the island where St. Herman lived his holy life and was afterward buried. I had been there once before, to attend St. Herman's August feast. The Liturgy for the feast was celebrated at the beautiful church of Ss. Sergius and Herman, a stone's throw from where the hermit lived. Pilgrims come annually from all over the world for the occasion, and there were so many clergy that the altar could not hold them all. So, the nave of the church became the altar and the large deck outside the church, the new nave. The rain stopped just as the priests emerged to offer Holy Communion to the faithful and resumed when they went back inside. After the Liturgy, we feasted on a delicious meal and gallons of hot coffee provided by the native Orthodox of the island. Bishops, priests, natives, and pilgrims all mingled happily together.

The spruce forest was alive with movement and sound, recalling the tiny villages within the Athonite monasteries—except that the walled defenses of Monk's Lagoon are its sea cliffs, upon which the mighty spruce stand as ever-vigilant sentries. The whole channel is a moat and gate which can be closed at any time by a stiff wind. The lagoon is a natural fortress. Once when welcoming a visitor St. Herman jokingly said, "Welcome to my castle." Yet there was a crucial difference between this natural castle and any monastery I had seen before, and the full gravity of it only hit me when I returned to the spot alone two months later and heard the silence.

After the August feast, everyone had gone home. Then, returning in the fall I was the only person for miles around, and the moss is such a velvety carpet that my footsteps made no sound on the path. This wasn't an eerie quiet but more like the expectant silence between one movement of a symphony and the next.

Everything in the chapels and outbuildings was kept in pristine condition, and when I step through the unlocked door of the chapel dedicated to the Kaluga Mother of God, it is as if the space has been waiting for me. The copy of the miracle-working icon was painted on Mount Athos on a canvas. It was then rolled up and shipped to a hermit who lived in Monk's Lagoon during the twentieth century. Our Lady is depicted not looking directly out of the icon but with eyes downcast, reading a book. I had never seen a depiction of her reading, but I knew without doubt she had opened it to Isaiah 7:14, "Therefore the Lord Himself will give you a sign: Behold, the virgin shall conceive and bear a Son, and shall call His name Immanuel." Her sash was tied above her belly; she was expecting. All in the chapel was expectation.

There are candles waiting to be lit on the chant stand alongside an akathist to the Kaluga icon. On the side table is a cutting board and a silver tray for *proskomidia*. A liturgical stole lies in readiness across the altar. If I had been a priest with prosphora and a blessing, the Liturgy would have practically served itself!

All three of the small chapels in Monk's Lagoon are thus—as if all the saints and angels had been chanting praises together just before I arrived and then leapt back into their icons the moment I stepped through the door.

The full import of this didn't dawn on me until I found the little cabin stocked full of food (man of the stomach that I am), bed made, oil lamps full, wood and kindling ready by the stove. At last it hit me: All of Monk's Lagoon is the enchanted castle of a fairy tale I had watched as a child with my brothers and sisters, where everything is waiting for the first guest to discover it—a wild, Alaskan *Beauty and the Beast*. First published in 1740 in French, the story was influenced by the ancient Greek tale "Cupid and Psyche," and in the film version, Belle walks past candlesticks, kettles, and clocks and feels as if they were animated just before she stepped into the room. She pauses to frown at a candlestick, certain that it had moved just a moment before. Feeling, like Rilke, that "there is no place that does not see you,"[4] I understood that this place where St. Herman had lived was the castle of my deepest longing.

---

4   R. M. Rilke and S. Mitchell, "Archaic Torso of Apollo," in *Ahead of All Parting: The Selected Poetry and Prose of Rainer Maria Rilke* (Random House Inc., 1995), 67.

In Disney's version, the French candlestick, Lumiere, welcomes Belle with a spectacular number, "Be Our Guest," as a feast is presented to her. The hospitality of the Beast's castle is not only welcome but sustaining, as it is on Mount Athos. It must be so because the pilgrim needs that time-honored shot of ouzo, the bite of loukoumi, and the strong Greek coffee to fortify himself, for he has come into the castle of his Lord. It must be so within those natural sea walls of St. Herman's castle, where dehydrated food and home-canned salmon are stacked by the woodstove.

The Lord bears no resemblance to Belle's Beast except symbolically—in fairy tales, this is the only way that matters. Namely, the castle and all within belong to Him. His presence is a fearful, consuming fire. And He is the Bridegroom—beautiful beyond hope—of every person's soul. Herein lies the secret of human longing for castles: It is not a desire for grand fortifications, but for a meeting with the King. But we dare not even acknowledge this great and terrible hope. So, we come to castles like tourists in Spain. I've been to the Alcázar de Segovia that inspired the iconic Disney castle. It is a museum, and I looked around with interest. But at last, to come to a living castle, and to be given such enchanting hospitality, how can one resist becoming a guest? How can one not join the Mother of God in her expectant silence?

This transition from stranger to guest is illustrated in the Lord's Parable of the Underdressed Wedding Guest. This is the rare parable that I think my generation may superficially understand better than the people of Christ's own time. In the parable, a man fails to wear the traditional wedding garment and is cast out of the feast. How many Millenials and Zoomers have showed up to a wedding wearing sweatpants and a hoodie? We do not know how to be guests anymore. We don't even bring our dishes to the sink. But we love fairy tales, even if Disney's version is the only one we know.

Saint John Chrysostom says that we weave our wedding garments with a virtuous life. But what if we have failed to master the spiritual Bassai Dai, and the passions still sit squarely on top of us? Don't despair! In Christ's time, a whole rack of wedding garments was freely offered to people as they arrived. First-century Jews had a veritable free Men's Wearhouse right outside the venue!

The feast is prepared and the table richly laden. The sinful, eleventh-hour yellow belts are welcomed alongside the spiritual black belts who punched, kicked, and fought their way into the castle from the first hour. If we could stay for a while and partake from that Table, we would be the Lord's own guests.

Then, one day, like Belle, we would find that we are no longer just guests. One day, we will see the unseen servants in their true, glorious forms: Our longing will be fulfilled, and we will become part of the Church. We realize that the Lord is not just Fearfully Awesome, He is also Love. And as this transition occurs from fear of God to love of God, there is a parallel joy, for the Lord has found our soul beautiful and wishes to have it as His Bride. We will find that we have not just entered the castle. The whole of it has been given to us.

2

THE FIFTY-FIVE-ACRE PLANET

KODIAK IS AT THE FAR end of Alaska's Emerald Chain; it is also at the very end of the supply chain, so often there are no eggs in Kodiak. If that happens, there are soon no eggs on Spruce Island, the island beyond the last island. The monks who live there are not overly troubled by this because they spend the majority of the year abstaining from eggs. In the shadow of their island lies yet a more remote, even more eggless island called St. Nilus. On this fifty-five-acre rock lives a small community of nuns.

I know the precise size because once, while the chaplain and I were trying to resurrect the ancient wood-splitting machine called Harold, we could not find the case of ratchet wrenches to loosen the spark plug. Just then a sister walked past.

"Where do you think it could be?" the chaplain asked her.

"I don't know. There are fifty-five acres, Papa," replied the sister, gesturing expansively.

Somewhere in those fifty-five acres there was a case of ratchets, but perhaps implied alongside this intelligence—which surely was not new to the chaplain, affectionately known as "Papa"—was that while that space is relatively small, it is rather too large to search when one's obedience is in the kitchen and there are only a few hours left before two o'clock lunch, and no eggs.

Indeed, circumnavigating the island in the monks' skiff, it seems like a tiny microcosm, and in winter, like a snow globe: complete with indistinct, black-robed figures moving through the whirling snowflakes. Yet, though I had entered the snow globe nearly a dozen times splitting wood with Harold (or with a maul when he chose to remain dead), it was as if the island were bigger on the inside. And though Papa gave me the tour around the whole place, I kept happening on landscapes that I had not seen, vistas new and different. I still lost my way.

It's bigger on the inside.

That phrase stands out to anyone who has ever watched BBC's *Doctor Who*, which concerns a time traveler in possession of a time machine shaped like a British police call box. From the outside it seems no bigger than a phone booth, but as he slips in the door, the camera shot switches to the inside of the deck of the spacecraft, and the viewer sees that the time machine is exceedingly large. These impossible dimensions are one of the most famous aspects of the show. That and, of course, the time-traveling adventures.

In like manner, I came to Spruce Island to stay nine days; as I write this, I have been here nine months. For Spruce, and for its little sister island St. Nilus, time seems to pass differently. On Spruce, Matins is served every day at 3 a.m., and if there is a festal liturgy as well, dawn will break when the chalice emerges from the altar. We sleep when it is bright out and wake under such a firmament of stars and such a blazing moon that silver light throws shadows on the bell as it is rung. The nuns do not discard names entrusted to them but keep them in prayer daily for the living and the dead.

Rather than travel through time, they enter into the mystical mystery of Christ's now.

Perhaps too the secret to the islands' timelessness is that they are so surrendered to time. On St. Nilus, creation groans. The Fall of God's intended order is felt on the serrated edge of the winter wind. The boom of the surf echoes without ceasing the Second Law of Thermodynamics: Everything is moving to a state of greater disorder. There is no illusion of permanence here. The sea gnaws ravenously at the fifty-five acres. Huge logs wash up on the running line of the skiff, trees crash onto roofs of buildings that blow away when not secured. All beams rot, sag, and eventually break.

Even a small tsunami would be a catastrophic event for this fifty-five-acre planet. This tiny, complete microcosm recalls Antoine de Saint-Exupéry's 1943 masterpiece in which "the little prince" constantly works against the catastrophic growth of the baobabs, which would burst under his tiny asteroid world.[5] In his travels to various similar planets, before reaching Earth, the little prince encounters many strange inhabitants. They are all quite mad, like the king without subjects or the businessman selling deeds to the stars. The prince finds all their doings frivolous, except for one: A lamplighter lights a single streetlamp every night, though his planet is so minuscule that one revolution takes only one minute. So, he is ever lighting and extinguishing his lamp.

In a similar vein, the nuns of St. Nilus are lighthouse keepers. There, in a pine-fragrant chapel, the uncreated light blazes like an unseen lighthouse beacon sustaining all the islands of the world and all the planets in the universe. The light we usually see comes from wax candles and a chandelier let down by a pulley. (Indeed,

---

5   Antoine de Saint-Exupéry, *The Little Prince* (Reynal & Hitchcock, 1943).

during a Christmastime Liturgy I saw it almost flatten an unwary sister passing beneath it.) It is a handmade, spartan affair of wood and chain. But behold, the wax catchers at the base of every candle are seashells from the beach. Each one is a pristine white rose petal from the sea, more gracefully curved than fine porcelain. In all my travels, even as far as the Great Lavra of Mount Athos, I have not found such a seashell chandelier.

Morning and evening, the nuns lower the chandelier. They light it and pull it up again to the heavens. Thus they grow old.

"Of all the men I met, the lamplighter's life alone seemed to have any meaning," said the little prince.

I was eleven years old when I finished reading *The Little Prince* for the first time. I was in a sunlit room when I read that the prince dies, and I saw the illustration of him falling to the desert ground.

He dies?!

I threw the book across the room and burst into tears. It didn't matter that he had gone elsewhere in spirit. A little prince visited our planet, and he died here.

Only, that is not the end of the matter. The archpastor of St. Nilus Skete is Bishop Maxim. His photograph, in which he raises the Holy Gifts, is hung from a great beam, salvaged from a wrecked ship, which now supports the refectory ceiling roof. This bishop, a world-renowned artist, painted a luminous portrait of the little prince, and on my first visit to St. Nilus I saw a copy of it in the nuns' library. Though short on space until a new building is completed, one of their cabins is still entirely dedicated to their library: They call it Bethlehem.

So there resides a little prince in Bethlehem.

From the library it is a short walk to the beautiful new building called Sinai; Papa's tour took us through its unfinished halls. One room on the first floor, perhaps a future office, is clearly the planning room. There is a phalanx of Post-it notes arrayed on the wall tracking a multitude of ongoing projects. Architectural schemas are rolled up or flattened on the table with weights, and there are large hardcover books with titles like *Cozy Convents* and *How to Build Your Own House in 30,000 Simple Steps*.

In a nook, though, I saw two slim volumes of C.S. Lewis's *The Chronicles of Narnia*.

Why were they there? Did a sister, daunted by the rising rows of neatly catalogued unfinished tasks, smuggle in the Oxford don to snatch a reprieve from reading *Plumbing: It's Not as Bad as You Think*? Or perhaps the two volumes were there as the leaven of the building—a dose of holy, nonlinear imagination that was just as necessary for the planners as the linear building plans. After all, building anything truly wonderful requires challenging the conventions of time and space, if only a little. The Pevensie children of the Narnia books found a world in a wardrobe.

I had looked for the world of Aslan when I visited the Wade Museum, which has one of C. S. Lewis's wardrobes. It was open, and, alas, my hand met the oak panel wall at the back. I confess there wasn't even real disappointment, because there had been no faith. Since reading *The Little Prince* in my boyhood, I had become more jaded. I did not even grimace in the museum; by then wardrobes had not led to Narnia for a while.

One day I came to St. Nilus Island to help carry an eight-hundred-pound woodstove into the newly constructed kitchen. Shortly before the skiff arrived carrying the stove, everyone went down to the beach to await it. We sat on the rocks looking out at the horizon. Unexpectedly, one of the nuns made a delightful reference to Puddleglum.

"He's the best character in the book!" I said. "Except for Aslan, of course, but he's the best character in all seven."

And everyone seemed gratified by this sentiment. The skiff arrived with two parishioners from the cathedral in Kodiak, men of prodigious physical intelligence. We all helped lift the stove, but they guided it and maneuvered through doorways with such composure that there was more ease in moving an eight-hundred-pound stove on a remote island than getting a refrigerator into a college dorm room. So great was the strength of these two men, I got the impression that if we all fell away under the stove's weight, they would bear it forward alone.

In forty minutes, the stove was in place, with not a single scratch on the hardwood floors. One sister said, "I've been dreading this for years, and just like that, it's done!"

As Papa passed out dried mango strips, a festive spirit spread over us. All fruit is a treat on the fifty-five-acre planet, and we munched merrily on the leathery, tangy, sweet fruit. We trooped down to the beach speaking with great animation about happy, inconsequential things. The sun sank low in the sky, casting golden-hour shadows on the sand. Soon, we pushed off the skiff of the Kodiak crew and watched the two men hop onto opposite sides of the boat and begin playfully rocking the vessel as it pulled away.

"It would be good to be that strong," said Papa.

A contented silence had stolen over me, and I did not say a word. Happy silence was so rare that I did not want to startle it away. When I looked down the beach, I saw the fathers were pulling in our skiff, and I hurried to join them. I took six steps before I heard a voice behind me.

"Are you leaving too? Stay with us!"

I stopped.

An unseen hand drew together a myriad of gleaming blessings, focusing them like lenses so that the diffuse radiance of grace suddenly gathered into a single shaft of light that pierced me through the heart.

I turned in the soft, low-tide sand.

In the slanting sunset, Papa and the company of nuns just stood there, smiling at me. It was a flat calm day; not even a zephyr played at the folds of their robes—the Angelic Order. I could barely look at them.

Stay.

Stay on the lamplighter's planet, stay in Narnia, stay to see time transcended. Stay at the home of all that is true from all the stories I love.

Oh, how I bowed to them.

"I'll come back," I said.

Since then, I've not thought of a better response than that. All that remains to say is that this light, which explodes from the pine-fragrant altar table of St. Nilus chapel, does not only sustain the universe. It also sharpens to a point, driving toward the hearts of all people. Those targets that the Divine Archer hits, He makes bigger. The light will not stop until the heart is larger than fifty-five acres, vaster than Narnia, bigger on the inside—spacious enough to contain the Kingdom of heaven.

WHEN THE GOD-MAN
MADE BREAKFAST

O NE DAY IN THE WHEATON College dining hall, my suite mate
was displeased with the cooking and held aloft a piece of fish
on his fork.

"What is wrong with this fish?" he asked.

"It's dead," I said, and everyone laughed.

Years later, I went fishing with the fathers of St. Michael's Skete.
I had heard about fishing from Scripture and was excited to haul in
the nets myself. Also, I was certain there would be plenty of oppor-
tunities for Bible jokes. Sure enough, out in the Gulf of Alaska,
hauling in the gill net was just what I expected. But the fish were
a surprise. Unlike my suite mate's fish, there was nothing wrong
with them; they were alive. Unlike the bug-eyed centerpiece of
the Costco seafood counter's frozen tableau, these huge sockeye
salmon insisted on life.

They tangled themselves in the net, flopped their muscular bodies, and rang the aluminum floor of the skiff with their heads, producing irregular gongs. Some are easily two feet long and can weigh up to twenty pounds. I had not counted on touching a living creature, especially not one that was so distressed, so full of the frantic will to live. Once the net was secured aboard, the fathers began to untangle the fish. Now the salmon excreted a pungent, frothy slime that made their bodies even more slippery. Yet even then they were beautiful.

I kept thinking of Gollum's riddle to Bilbo:

Alive without breath,
As cold as death;
Never thirsty, ever drinking,
All in mail never clinking.[6]

Their silver scales really looked like gleaming suits of armor, perfectly designed to serve each creature better than even the finest coat of Morian mithril. These salmon, though, weren't "ever drinking." The fathers sliced across their gills with a small blade. Initially, I thought this was to mercy-kill them, but in fact it is to bleed the fish, which are then placed headfirst into a bucket.

I wondered whether their lives were protracted by the bucket until the oxygen in the bloody water was used up. Even though I knew that they were not sentient, that their suffering lacked the awareness that their short lives were ebbing away, the process was still brutal. Of course, all these thoughts amplified my timidity

---

6   J. R. R. Tolkien, *The Hobbit; Or, There and Back Again* (Ballantine, 1984), 83–84.

and my distance from this primal, apostolic occupation. I was in the monks' way. I was worse than useless. My breathing shallow, I stood flatfooted and out of balance with the gently rocking skiff.

Yet despite the carnage, completing a successful haul and pulling aboard almost a score of huge salmon was always an exhilarating cause for celebration. Once, Presvytera Mary spotted a jumper, a member of a school of salmon who for sheer joy of life leaps clear out of the water for a moment. The jumper was right in our cove. When we realized their size—that they were too long to be pink salmon and were not speckled like them—the mood became electric; we had never caught silvers in Sunny Cove before.

"But give the word, Father!" I said to Fr. Andrew, who was at the helm.

I only asked permission to add to the drama. I knew he would not pass up a chance for silver-studded fishing history. Already, he was ghosting us toward the little school, and we played out our net ever so sweetly. We cast it in a wide circle that tightened as we heaved it back in. That day we caught eighteen mighty silvers as long as my arm. Father Andrew congratulated Presvytera Mary for spotting the first jumper. The monks never failed to have a catch when she was aboard.

"It is the Lord," she said in the exact words of John, the beloved disciple, when he recognized the risen Christ on the beach. I almost fell overboard myself in my haste to turn to her husband, whose name is none other than Fr. Peter.

"Spring into the sea, Father!" I said to him, so excited. "Spring!"

Father Peter blinked, unsure if I was kidding. The silence that often greets my Bible jokes lengthened—though for a second I really believed he was considering jumping into the water in solidarity with his patron saint.

Finally I said, "I understand, Father, the Apostle Peter was stripped for work, but you are in fishing gear, so you do not have to spring into the sea when the Lord comes."

"You know your Scriptures well, Anthony," he said with a smile.

By the time we checked the halibut line—our initial mission—it was too late in the evening to process the fish. The next day, a local Orthodox fisherman sold dozens of red salmon to Fr. Andrew at wholesale cannery prices. It was time for a fish-processing party.

The morning following, we came to the nuns' island, St. Nilus, bearing our plastic totes full of rigid red and silver salmon. The sisters came out to meet us on the beach with brand-new gutting knives and nonslip fish-grabbing gloves. The rude plywood tables were brought below the tideline, and the sushi chef mats were spread open on them. Both monastic communities were out in force. A spirit of excitement reigned, which I felt despite my dread of the imminent gore. We had been blessed with plenty, the sun was shining, and the otters were cavorting offshore. It was as near to a golden day of harvest as I had ever been.

So, I was determined that this time I would contribute beyond just rinsing fillets. Since filleting itself is an art that takes time to learn, the only thing left to do was to disembowel the fish. The chaplain of St. Nilus was assigned to teach me this indelicate process.

He showed me how to hold the slippery silver steady with my gloved hand and saw off the head with the other. Papa saw how thoroughly uncomfortable and pale I was during this demonstration.

"You have all this stuff inside you too, you know," he said to set me at ease.

"No, I don't!" I said with a hysterical note in my voice. "I'm functionally gnostic!"

After paring away the fins, the final cut from the back fin to the headless front unzips the fish like a scaly ziplock bag, exposing the congealed viscera within. The moment of maximal horror was at hand; I had seen the fathers do this part, but nothing could have prepared me to reach inside and close my naked fingers on a fistful of clammy, slimy, oozy fish guts.

Squish.

My brain fritzed with revulsion then totally shorted out as I ripped out the heart, intestines, spleen, and those nebulous white fat pockets. I inhaled the rank smell of all the offal ripening in the sun. I threw the mess to the gathering eagles, gulls, and crows. At some point, I splatted a fish too hard on the table, and the nasty strand of a giblet covered in intestinal juice flew up and caught me in the face. A wounded dog's yip escaped my throat.

"You poor guy," a sister said.

"You've never pitied me before when I've gotten splashed!" teased one of the monks working next to me.

I am notoriously squeamish, and already I had begun to feel lightheaded and nauseated. In the belly of one fish were half a dozen tiny fish. *Its babies?* I wondered. *No, fish aren't mammals.* Then it hit me just how savage fallen creation is: This salmon had just eaten these fish, and before it even had a chance to digest them, we caught it.

Yet despite the grim work, that harvest-time spirit that I had initially felt kept motivating me. I had never seen the monks and nuns joking and working together so happily. It was focused, tough labor but also somehow relaxed. Also, on this occasion I was the only pilgrim, and I felt privileged to be accepted among the monastics as a fellow participant in this ancient ritual of the homecoming fishermen. So I decided that at worst I would either faint, hurl, or both. After all, the sand was soft to collapse on, and puke would hardly be out of place among the discarded guts. These were people I trusted, not just with my life—I trust plenty of people with that—but, way harder, my embarrassment. Of course, the fathers would never have let me live it down if I'd passed out, but their teasing would not have been mean and humiliating.

However, I remembered my dad's advice for staying on my feet. He is a general surgeon, and my six-foot-four height comes from him. Recalling the exercises he gave me as a kid, I began to tighten and relax the muscles in my legs. Shuffling in the sand, I activated my calves by standing on my tiptoes. The blood shot back into my brain, which, after the third handful of giblets tossed to the carrion birds, started freaking out about it less. I began to compete with the filleting fathers by seeing how many gutted salmon I could pile in front of them before they had a chance to finish their current spine.

Time passed quite quickly once I got going. With the rising tide at our heels, we rinsed out the totes and put the fillets in them. We splashed and scrubbed down the tables with sea water, then carried them up the beach. I took off my beslimed glove and rubbed my hands raw with saltwater and sand. I had not passed out or thrown up.

By the end of those few hours, I was a little less gnostic and a little more functional. To crown it all, it was Homemade Pizza Day in the nuns' refectory. For someone as woozy as I was earlier, my appetite recovered marvelously when I smelled the melting cheese with little pieces of smoked salmon on it in lieu of pepperoni. Everyone found a spot on a bench or the stairs, and we ate without even taking off our fishing bibs. We talked and laughed, and I was not just a pilgrim but part of this sacred little world. Of all the lovely meals I've enjoyed on St. Nilus with a finely set table, a formal ring of the bell, and spiritual writings read and discoursed upon, no meal stands out more sweetly in my memory than the paper-plate informality of that harvest day.

Of course, Papa was right; whether I accept it or not, I have organs like the salmon I eat. Likewise, I am mortal, and one day a bigger fish will get me with that salmon still undigested in my stomach. Yet being mortal was changed forever by the Incarnation. By becoming Man, the Lord made having a gut a means of drawing closer to Him because He had a gut.

After the Apostle Peter sprang into the sea—and then presumably put some clothes on—he and the other disciples found Christ had prepared breakfast for them on the beach. The God-Man made breakfast. There was toast. Additionally, the Gospel says there were fish on the coals even before the disciples brought fish from their own catch.

Where did the Lord get those fish? Surely He did not need to order them to come; they would have come of themselves to their Creator, in joy to be prepared by Him, to be consumed by Him. What greater destiny could there be for a fish?

A couple millennia later, there was a similar fish breakfast after the Feast of the Annunciation with my seminary classmates and our aforementioned professor of ethics, Dr. Timothy Patitsas. After we feasted on fish and chips, we were well contented.

"The fish rejoices to find its *telos*[7] in being reunited with the Eucharist inside our stomachs," Dr. Tim mused, calm, as if commenting on the weather.

At the time I thought the comment was a little weird, and I might have forgotten it. But one of my wiser classmates looked stunned.

"Dr. Tim, how do you just come up with these things?" he asked.

In my introduction to this book, I mentioned the years-long journey of the salmon, who unerringly return across thousands of miles to the place they were hatched. Dr. Patitsas's comment reveals the

---

7   Greek for "purpose" or "ultimate end."

mystery of why the salmon come back. If their Little Entrance is their entry into the narthex of Sunny Cove on Spruce Island, their Great Entrance is being caught, offering themselves after the pattern of their Creator as nourishment for us. Native American traditions of gratitude to the fallen animals they've hunted reveal the paradox that though the animals want to live, they also freely offer themselves as a sacrifice. This love of life and self-offering exist at the same time and indeed are inextricable. The salmon love Life, the God-man Jesus Christ, and give their lives to return to Him in our bellies, feeding us along the way. That silver salmon in the cove did not have to jump, but in its joy at being a salmon, it let us, the fishermen, know it was there.

One time on the skiff, I made an inane joke at the salmon's expense.

"Don't insult the fish," said Fr. Andrew. "They feed us. We need to be respectful."

A monk with tough, sandpaper hands, when Fr. Andrew brings down a club on the head of a huge, eighty-pound halibut, it does not flop again. With long, deft strokes he wields the fillet knife, slicing free every edible ounce from the white fish, leaving only the parasite-ridden stomach. I kiss that hand; he is our priest.

On the next morning his rubber bibs are exchanged for a stole, and the knife for a lance. The solar-powered battery cells only have enough juice to power one freezer, so from the same freezer the halibut are kept in, a carefully wrapped prosphora loaf has been brought up to the chapel to thaw. Before the Liturgy begins, Fr. Andrew's same calloused hands perform the Office of the Holy Oblation. Those selfsame hands with greatest reverence bear the Gifts in the Great Entrance all the way through the royal doors to the altar table. Soon after, at the climax of the Liturgy, he lifts high the paten and the chalice, offering not just the bread and the wine upon them but, invisibly, that same halibut from yesterday, all halibut, all creation.

"Your own of Your own, we offer to You on behalf of all and for all."

This mystical participation in the Lord's Last Supper is the summit of our lives. The Lord loves us body and soul, and, knowing our needs, he also provides breakfast for us after Liturgy. Indeed, sometimes breakfast is all too present in my mind, especially because the house chapel of St. Michael's Skete is on the second floor above the kitchen. There have been times when a most delicious aroma has wafted up from the oven, causing stomachs to rumble during the anaphora. To avoid this and to serve the meal in a timely fashion, Fr. Adrian, the cook, has developed careful scheduling. Right after receiving Communion, he goes down and begins to grill.

After the prayers of thanksgiving are read, we chant the psalms "What Shall I Render to the Lord?" and "O Give Thanks unto the Lord." We are waiting for Fr. Andrew to finish consuming the Gifts and for Fr. Adrian to ring the little bell announcing that the meal is served. When we hear that sound, Fr. Andrew comes forth from the altar in his best cassock and his festive wool *kalimafi*.[8] The youngest pilgrim is given the icon of the day's feast and leads the procession downstairs. The fathers follow, then the brethren, and often we chant the best of St. Herman's five stichera, which begins with a paraphrase of the saint's own exhortation:

What is above all, if not the Lord our Creator, Adorner of beauty, Giver of Life, Maintainer and Nourisher of all things: is it not Him that it is befitting to love, as most worthy of love,

---

8   A liturgical hat.

and to place one's happiness in Him, thus, O saint, didst thou teach; likewise teach us also with all our heart to love God.[9]

For a short procession down a single flight of stairs, there's a tremendous amount of joy in it. I try to ignore the food as we near the table but often fail. Each plate is so pleasing to behold, with a salad of glowing beets set off against the forest-green kale and golden potatoes. But the eye is drawn to the salmon. Father Adrian has spent twenty-five years perfecting his salmon-grilling technique. He pulls off the steaks just as trace amounts of glistening white fat begin to stream from them. Only minimal seasoning is required because the flavor is as vivid as the color. Alaskan salmon is nothing like the anemic pink of a restaurant salmon in the Lower Forty-Eight, frozen for an eon before being microwave-thawed. No, the fish being served is the vibrant, ruby-red Chinook, the King Salmon, that was swimming in Sunny Cove yesterday. This morning he's on his joyous way to be united with the Eucharist in our bellies.

Now the icon is being placed on its stand, and Fr. Andrew takes his place at the head of the table. The seat where he presides over the meal is almost directly beneath the altar table one floor above him. Hats come off, and he raises his hand once more to trace the sign of the cross over the long, richly laden table.

The food is blessed.

"Jesus said to them, 'Come *and* eat breakfast'" (John 21:12).

---

9   *Saint Herman of Alaska: His Life and Service* (St. Herman of Alaska Brotherhood, 2009), 30.

4

ⷲHE WARREN OF BELL AND BOWL

ᴀᴛ Sᴛ. Mɪᴄʜᴀᴇʟ's Sᴋᴇᴛᴇ ᴏɴ St. Herman's Spruce Island, it
should not be surprising that the most common names I
encountered were Herman and Michael. At one point there were so
many Hermans that we playfully numbered them. It was Herman
1 who led my first expedition up Mount St. Herman. Indeed, I have
yet to climb the mountain without a Herman. This one was anxious
to try a new route—one that he pioneered but that lacked a beaten
path—with orange paracord markers that one of the fathers had
hung from the boughs of the spruces to mark the path.

After we traversed a barbed-wire fence and I wiped out on a
stretch of wet vegetation, we proceeded upward until we became
lost. It was only with the encouragement of Herman 1, Herman 2,
and a third brother that I did not give up on reaching the summit.

Unlike the mist, my irritability dissipated on reaching the great
steel, three-bar Russian cross that the coast guard had helicoptered
to the peak. There's a red transponder light at the top that serves as
their beacon and as ours. Below us, the enshrouding cloud hid the

surrounding islands and sea but stopped short of covering the plateau on which we stood. Here various species of moss proliferated, their shades of green vivid on the sunless day. The air was pristine, almost sweet, encouraging deep, lung-slaking breaths. Sharp, fanned edges of shale punctured the surface like half-submerged shards of a giant's obsidian dagger. There were no spruce trees here, just the cross. It was an otherworldly space—the closest I have come to being in the eye of a hurricane.

After we chanted hymns together and spent time alone in silence, there was one more thing I wanted to do. From my pocket I fished out a damp piece of notepaper covered in a hastily scrawled quotation. Herman 2 sang with me, Herman 1 provided the *ison*, and the other brother looked on dubiously as we sang,

Far over, the misty mountains cold
To dungeons deep and caverns old
We must away ere break of day
To seek the pale enchanted gold.[10]

On the way down I fell no fewer than four times, but I was in much better spirits. The whole expedition took four hours. A few weeks later, Herman 3 went on a solo run up the marked trail and clocked in at a total of one and a half hours. Later, I was given the task to guide Herman 4 to the top, but he was a former coast guard and a big-game hunter. This meant he could somehow watch the horizon and at the same time read the signs of the ground. He definitely did not need me to guide him, especially since I stumble if I take my eyes off the trail for a second to look for the next paracord. It was he who pointed out the land otter in the far trees, though all

---

10   Tolkien, *The Hobbit*, 27–28.

I saw was a blur. However, near the top he called me to look up in time to see a white rabbit before it disappeared into its burrow.

I had only seen white rabbits in captivity on the property immediately adjacent to the forty-acre, family-owned organic farm I worked at in Florida a couple years ago. They were suspended in individual cages above the ground, and when I walked past, a couple rabbits would inevitably startle, have nowhere to run, and crash frantically about their tiny cages. This would in turn startle dozens of other rabbits who then crashed frantically about their tiny cages. Every day picking strawberries involved a dissonant progression of cacophonous cages. Then, each rabbit would become perfectly still—except for its racing heart—and regard us out of a single violet, inbred eye.

"Their life isn't so bad. They have shade and food and their own space," I said to a friend and fellow worker on the farm one day. Though surely jolted by the alarming, multilayered stupidity of that comment, she recovered quickly.

"It's so unnatural! They're hanging above the ground. They're *burrowers*. They love to dig."

Later when I read *Watership Down* at the skete, I found out that a rabbit burrow with its wild, underground network of tunnels, caverns, exits, and entrances is called a warren. As usual, when I learned a new word, it started to show up in my life.

Indeed, I might have predicted that I would hear it during a classic dishwashing discourse with Herman 2. The creek water, heated on the wood stove and poured steaming into two tubs in the sink, both stimulates the circulation in the dishwasher's hands and turns the turbines of theological thought.

That day I was holding forth on how the Walla Walla Roastery in Washington seems to be spiritually connected with St. Michael's Skete in Alaska. When I visited the coffee roastery, outside it hung a bell made by a bellmaker who now lives in Kodiak, who also forged the bell that hangs outside The Meeting of the Lord Chapel in Monk's Lagoon. Furthermore, the roastery was built by Thomas Reese, who holds the all-time record for the most frequent pilgrim to Spruce Island. He sends us coffee on the feasts in bright blue packaging, and its fragrance permeates the skete when we brew it. Its taste is of such a magnitude finer than our common coffee that the monks know the Washington roasts at a sip. So, there is a coffee, bell, and pilgrim connection between the roastery and the skete. But typical of those daring dishwashing discourses, I reached for something more.

It seemed to me—and it could have just been my fancy—that during my visit there was a deeper resonance between the very space of the roastery and the space of the skete. It was as if the sound of the bell, the smell of the coffee, and the presence of my guide, who was the brother of Thomas Reese, all contributed to a whole that was greater than the sum of its parts—the same whole in which St. Michael's Skete was also participating. It was like they were on the same spiritual frequency. When I tried to articulate this to Herman 2, he understood at once. This Herman often approaches a subtle subject with allusive sentence fragments that I am unable to reproduce because I cannot remember them. I could no more replicate the seemingly careless flick of a Zen calligrapher's brush. The dumbed-down gist is:

"And does that surprise you? That a man who loves St. Michael's Skete would build that love into the walls of his roastery?"

It does surprise me because I am functionally a materialist. I often forget even the axiomatic truth that the creation of an artist can turn numinous, precipitating the beholder into an encounter with the Uncreated Energies of God ordering all things. It stretches me to my limit to consider that the structure of a building could hold grace in its very walls. It seems incredible that the holiness of matter, sustained constantly by the Uncreated Light, is revealed through the priestly hand of an artist.

However, I had encountered the fingerprints of the Creator before, and I could not ignore them this time. It happens whenever I meet a master artist. I am constantly reminded of one such master's work as I put away the bowls in the kitchen.

His name is David Young, the Lion Potter of Gettysburg. After befriending his son, who also worked on the aforementioned farm, I visited the whole family in Pennsylvania on my drive back up to Boston. David let me sit in his studio and watch as he bent over the spinning wheel. Without any of the vivifying lightning of Dr. Frankenstein, David's fingers hovered above the clay. I watched as the Lion Potter stroked it, and I saw the mug bloom between his forefinger and thumb. It was as if his hand called forth from the clay a longing for form it did not know it had. Then another lump was cast upon the wheel, and a mug rose forth from it again. Then it happened again.

As Marcus Aurelius once said, "It loved to happen."[11]

Soon there was a full flight of eighteen mugs on a board. His wife, Junko, makes the handles, and they are graceful enough to give a swan pause. Her Japanese cooking is of such exquisite, nourishing caliber that it seems only right that it be contained in the bowls of a master potter. When it was mealtime at the Youngs' house, it was my singular pleasure to choose my bowl from the cupboard.

But at St. Michael's Skete we have six stoneware bowls made in China and donated by a defunct convent, five soup bowls with factory-scalloped edges, eight Amazon Basics–style soup bowls,

---

11   Marcus Aurelius, *Meditations* X.12, quoted in J. D. Salinger, *Franny and Zooey* (Back Bay Books/Little, Brown and Company, 1991), 149.

four larger bowls, and four wooden bowls. They all stack in a very specific way on the shelf. I would not spare them a thought, much less catalog them here, except for contrast. When I had opened the cupboard above the counter at the Youngs' house, I found myself in Ali Baba's Cave of Wonders.

Instead of rubies or emeralds lining the shelves, there were bowls dipped in hand-mixed glazes that surpassed the glow of jewels. For instance, there are at least three greens: Dragon Rider, Lotus, and Wintergreen. (The only greens that can match them are found in Spruce Island mosses.) These colors each adorn a bowl that is at once wholly unique in all the world and yet uniform in its fidelity to God's intent for bowls.

David has been throwing bowls for over forty years, and he consciously tries to make each one lovelier than the last. Once, earlier in his career, he was dissatisfied with his technique, so he locked himself in the basement and did nothing but throw bowls for two and a half years. Though they have never met, the retired bellmaker of Kodiak is his spiritual kinsman. The two of them have the same longing for the Beautiful.

The bellmaker and his wife often offer their home as a way point, a place of rest to pilgrims traveling to and from St. Michael's Skete. After returning from Walla Walla, I stayed a night with them. He described how every time he begins work on a new project, there is this great excitement.

This time, he thinks, *I am going to capture it.*

The huge family of bells outside St. Silouan Orthodox Church in Walla Walla are his children. The largest, a twelve-hundred-pound bell, is monolithic without being monstrous; it is meek in its very immensity by never being anything more than a bell. It rings, the whole of it, with a deep, majestic timbre the townspeople can feel in their toes.

Conversely, the bell outside the Meeting of the Lord Chapel on Spruce Island is not heavier than thirty pounds. Last summer, I was surprised when Fr. Andrew let a visiting group of children in Monk's Lagoon hammer away at it. Yet, he knew its special virtue: As many times as it was asked by the reckless yanking of the rope, it answered with that same high but robust, sweet but resounding note. In Monk's Lagoon buildings have disintegrated, wooden crosses on cupolas have crumbled, but the bell speaks the same name every time.

The bellmaker's creations were not just for churches adorned with reliefs of saints. He had made bells covered in bronze bunches of grapes for vineyards, one covered with honeybees alighting on flowers for an apiary, and one for the Walla Walla Coffee Roastery.

During each creative journey with a piece, the bellmaker must painstakingly sacrifice the infinite potentiality of everything it might have been in favor of one simple thing that is. No matter how it turns out, he is bitterly disappointed. Like David, who strives to make each bowl more beautiful than the last, each man knows he has fallen short despite his mastery.

In the Lion Potter's gallery, when someone accidentally breaks a vessel to pieces, David always shrugs and says, "It's just clay." Thus is the potter's glory greater than the alchemist's: His material never ceases to be clay, but by taking the form of a bowl it draws out the dignity of all clay.

Before the bowl shattered, I saw it. I saw matter hold grace.

Back in the kitchen with Herman, I've stopped wiping down counters because I'm so excited that there is a real way the very walls of Walla Walla Roastery are linked with the walls of St. Michael's Skete. Thomas Reese built like the monks built. His love for them and Spruce Island is expressed spiritually and physically in the roastery. Their work is intertwined just as the bellmaker's and the Lion Potter's are.

"It really is like different planets!" I said, missing the mark.

"A warren," corrected Herman.

No more cages suspended above the ground; instead, a warren, deep enough to tunnel from Alaska to Washington, from Washington to Pennsylvania. The way through the labyrinth isn't marked with orange paracord. Instead, the smell of coffee, the ring of a bell, or the space of a bowl silently intimate that the entrance to the warren is near at hand. However, passing into the warren often requires more than noticing the strange, gratuitous loveliness of roasted beans, bells, and bowls.

Once at the farm, I had displayed some of David's bowls on a table in the common area called the Honey House. The head farmer's nine-year-old daughter ran through the Honey House but pulled up short when she saw the bowls.

"Those are beautiful," she said.

I felt so delighted—so vindicated that this child who runs constantly and so rarely used three-syllable words had been arrested by the bowls—that I missed my chance.

"Yes! They really are!" I cried.

If only I had remained calm I might have asked her, "Why are they beautiful?" Then I might know the answer to the inscrutable riddle that every bowl and bell poses.

Most of the time it is enough that the bowl is pretty, but sometimes on a quiet summer night we know that its beauty is permeable—that if we just whirled around when the bowl was not expecting it, we would catch it as an arched gate to the warren.

Yet if it is an entrance riddle, in what language is it spoken? Who but a child could hope to speak in a tongue of bronze or shaped clay? Who but a created thing could know a created thing?

"It's a wonderful thing to be clay in God's hands," David said once.

Both he and the bellmaker are fractals of their own work. Like the potter's clay, the bellmaker reached upward toward a Beauty he could not name. Straining like a blooming mug on the wheel for the caress of the Divine Finger, he gave shape to the upside-down bowl of a bell.

Like the bellmaker's rivulet of molten tin, David pours himself into his work, casting his substance as an alloy of focus, prayer, and hope so that each bowl will be more beautiful than the last. So the one pours bowls, and the other throws bells—vessels of food, vessels of music—and thus both men themselves become vessels, formed of longing.

They recall Peter S. Beagle's line, "Your name is a golden bell hung in my heart, and I would tear myself to pieces to hear it said once."[12]

As creatures of clay, these men are themselves capable of being broken. The bellmaker almost destroyed his lungs with the fumes of craft. David has grown old shaping clay so that it takes all his strength and discipline to continue throwing bowls. They spent themselves for the Beautiful until they themselves bear cracks from the strain. "A broken and a contrite heart—[This], O God, You will not despise" (Ps. 51:17). This broken humility seems to be the necessary step for ringing the golden bell within the heart. The thousands of shattered potsherds are a kind of analogous repentance breaking the hard wall of pride around the heart. Then at last, amid the ruins of countless failures, a worthy bell or bowl is formed, and the maker finds a grace unlooked for—that in the struggle, the casings of his pride have also fractured. Shining through the cracks is the golden bell with a name that answers all riddles, unlocks all doors.

---

12 Peter S. Beagle, *The Last Unicorn: 40th Anniversary Edition* (Roc, 2008), 12.

Twice, a girl called Alice happened into the Wonderland of Lewis Carroll's mind. Once she tumbled down the rabbit hole following a white rabbit, and once she fell through a looking glass. Her travels, mapping the warren of Lewis Carroll's imagination, are contained in two slim volumes which have formed the backbone of imaginative literature in the West for the last two hundred years.

If that warren, so terrible, confounding, and wonderful, was a creation of Lewis Carroll, consider how much more awesome is the Warren of Bell and Bowl, which contains Carroll's warren and all other creative warrens. It is opened by a name hung like a bell in the heart.

5

THE BATTLE HYMN OF OCTAVIUS GRINSWALD

A T MY FIRST FESTAL LUNCH at St. Michael's Skete, the reading did not last the whole meal. Father Andrew rang a little bell, and one of the fathers kissed the icon of Panagia, got a blessing, and sat down. Then Fr. Andrew welcomed the pilgrims and asked each of us what we did. When I told him that I taught and loved English Language Arts, he asked if I had anything I could recite for the company.

Be still my heart! A soliloquy for the celibates, a fête for the fathers, a play for the pilgrims! Yet all that came to mind was . . .

"Life's but a walking shadow, a poor player that struts and frets his hour upon the stage!"

No, no, *Macbeth* would never do here, in an Alaskan July where the sun shines for eighteen hours a day. I was blanking on everything. Then, I remembered something, though it was a mad gamble. I had to chance it! They were so courteous; they would have appreciated anything, but I wanted to dazzle them. I wanted them to love me. So that was the day I told the Holy Synods of two monasteries about an episode of *Star Trek: The Next Generation.*

Starfleet was just recovering from a brutal war with the Cardassian Empire, and the truce was fragile. Then Jean-Luc Picard, that great captain of the flagship of Starfleet, the *Enterprise,* receives an urgent communiqué from high command. He must intercept and stop at all costs a rogue Starfleet captain who is attacking and destroying Cardassian vessels in deep space in violation of the treaty!

The rogue captain refuses to stand down, and Picard is forced to put the *Enterprise* on red alert, arming all photon torpedoes to fire upon another ship in their own fleet. Just before they give terrible battle, one of Picard's men, Transporter Chief O'Brien, asks leave to sneak through the enemy shields to reason with the rogue captain. O'Brien had served with him and knew that the man was grieving his two children, whom the Cardassians had murdered in a planetary attack.

Picard grants permission to O'Brien, who beams over to his old captain unarmed. Instead of trying to convince him through force of argument, he reminds him of an old song they used to sing under his command. A song that the captain had always liked. They begin to sing it together.

Many years after seeing the episode, I was shocked that I remembered the first line of that song. The first line was followed by the second, until, to my delight, the whole stanza stood shining in my mind. More than a recalling from within, it was like the song was out there somewhere, and it poured itself into my consciousness. The words were too resonant with age for the showrunner, Gene Roddenberry, to have written them. I looked the song up. It's an old

Scottish lay, oft sung at the funerals of soldiers to this day. It goes like this:

> The Minstrel-Boy to the war is gone,
>> In the ranks of death you'll find him;
> His father's sword he has girded on,
>> And his wild harp slung behind him.
> "Land of Song!" said the warrior-bard,
>> "Tho' all the world betrays thee,
> One sword, at least, thy rights shall guard,
>> One faithful harp shall praise thee!"
> The Minstrel fell!—but the foeman's chain
>> Could not bring his proud soul under;
> The harp he loved ne'er spoke again,
>> For he tore its chords asunder;
> And said, "No chains shall sully thee,
>> Thou soul of love and bravery!
> Thy songs were made for the pure and free,
>> They shall never sound in slavery."[13]

I sang it to the monks and nuns that day and was glad. "Warrior Bard," the song calls him. What could be a greater profession than that?

Of course, the first and only *Dungeons & Dragons* character of my life was a human bard, whom I named Octavius Grinswald. Our campaign took place in the second semester of seminary. As Grinswald, I gave my heraldic proclamation, "I draw my sword." And "I sing a song of courage!"

---

13   Thomas Moore, *Poetry of Thomas Moore* (Macmillan, 1903), 30–31.

It gave a "plus two" attack boost to all my allies.

Octavius Grinswald died in a labyrinth deep underground holding off a six-armed stone golem so that his friends could escape. The last thing they heard was his song, cut off abruptly by some vicious golemic onslaught as they rode the stone elevator to the safety of the sunlit world. Octavius had papers to write, chapel to attend, and his evening shift at the library.

That might have been the end of Octavius Grinswald, except that during my stay at the monastery, two bears swam from Kodiak to Spruce Island to investigate the fragrance of the Ouzinkie village dump. The fathers of St. Michael's Skete, three and a half miles away, noted it because bears had not been seen on Spruce Island for over a decade. Then news came that two additional bears had been spotted. Shortly thereafter a nun arrived to visit the skete.

Since she was staying at a neighbor's home at the foot of the hill, there was a non-zero chance that one of the bears might roam over to our borough and cross her path.

"We should probably send someone to walk her up," said Fr. Andrew at *trapeza*[14] the day before. "Someone with a loud voice."

And he looked at me with a smile. Leave it to Fr. Andrew to find a mission profoundly suitable for my stats. He had no illusions about my ability to defeat a bear in single combat, but he knew that I have a loud voice and that if I sang, this might frighten the bears away, if indeed one were abroad, hungry for a visiting nun. Resurrect Octavius! It's time for the Warrior Bard.

So twenty-five minutes before 3 a.m. Matins, I took up a hiking pole in my right hand and a large electric lantern in my left. At the threshold of the skete, I intoned the *apechema,* a vocal tuning into

---

14 The Greek word for "table." The fathers used this word to denote both the dining hall and/or the event of the meal itself.

the strange scale—three syllables sung across the structural notes of the mode.

Aaaananaeeeee!

Oh no, we're in First Mode now, boys! This ain't *do-re-mi* land no more. Save that Julie Andrews stuff for the sunlit lands. It's a Byzantine night, with eight ancient modes and three ancient scales. The microtonal difference between an Eastern and Western scale gives an evocative strangeness to the pitches of First Mode. They blow over the familiar spruce trees like an incongruous desert wind, turning the island I thought I knew into one where there is a non-zero chance of bears and stone golems with six arms.

At the top of my lungs, gloriously interrupting the prayer rules of the brethren, I sang the Troparion of the Cross. First in Greek—and Greek never sounded better, with those pure syllables sharp on the downbeat as drawn swords. Then in Albanian, then English. My three holy languages. Over and over, I cycled this song of courage:

Save, O Lord, Thy People and bless Thine inheritance; grant victory to the faithful against the adversaries of the faith. And protect Thy people, by the power of Thy Cross.[15]

My liturgics professor called this hymn our fight song, because at Holy Cross Greek Orthodox School of Theology we sing it before sporting events. We also learned that "adversaries of the faith" was a euphemism for "barbarians" in the Greek. The ancient hymn originally prays for the king to be victorious over the invading barbarian hordes. The professor was pointing out that it had been the actual fight song of the Byzantines in Constantinople, whose

---

15 "Hymns of the Feast of the Exaltation of the Cross." Greek Orthodox Archdiocese of America. Accessed August 1, 2025. https://www.goarch.org/-/hymns-of-the-feast-of-the-exaltation-of-the-cross.

warriors were beset for centuries by enemies much more terrifying than the St. John's Catholic basketball team—those smooth-cheeked barbarians!

So, at last, Octavius Grinswald strides forth in real life, I thought. I should have asked the visiting sister if she felt a plus-two attack buff as she made her way out of the house. Together, we walked up to the skete. I was still singing and peering into every shadow outside the umbral sphere of my lantern. It was the phial of Galadriel, Cate Blanchett's version of the character, with the ethereal voice: "And to you, Anthony Linderman, I give a fluorescent lantern, our brightest bulb. May it be a light for you in dark places, when all other lights go out."

Oh, I felt as if I could spend a lifetime escorting nuns up hills. With my opposable thumbs I would jab the eyes of any bear that attacked. I would armbar that thing; against my Brazilian Jiu Jitsu, he would tap out. And when I inevitably died a horrible death and got eaten, the nun would be safe at the skete, telling them all how brave I was.

It's a mistake, though, to see the troparion as a battering ram, or even an aegis of protection. That's just the warrior side—a sword in the hand, a cross that impales the enemy on the vertical axis. The enemy ascends the cross, ready or not. However, the horizontal crossbar of the hilt also represents the outspread arms of the Lord, embracing all people. This is the bardic aspect of the Warrior Bard, who offers himself in performance for everyone. He who would empty himself cannot pick and choose. Either he sings with all his heart, even for his enemies, or he fails in his vocation. If he rejects or resents even a single person, his offering is incomplete, and that empty spot where that person should be in the bard's heart is the broken link to Christ's grace.

The reason I told the story of the *Star Trek* episode before singing that song is that it gives the piece its rightful context of self-offering. O'Brien pours it out like a libation for his captain. They sing together:

"Land of Song,
    Tho' all the world betrays thee,
One sword, at least, thy rights shall guard."

But O'Brien sings the last line by himself: "One faithful harp shall praise thee."

The two men sit in silence for a moment. O'Brien has become that one faithful harp, the only man in Starfleet who really understands the captain's bereavement at the hands of his enemies. Then the captain says, "I'm not gonna win this one, am I, chief?"

"No, sir."

And he surrenders to Picard.

Strange, that a warrior's ballad convinced the captain to surrender. Yet, it was more than a martial song, just as the Troparion of the Cross is more than a martial hymn. When sung by the true Warrior Bard, the song and the singer are both the offering. He knows that to chant that hymn, he must be willing to die outside the gates of Constantinople, shielding her from the barbarian horde. The strength behind his stand is motivated by love of the city, not hatred of the enemy. The highest description of a soldier is that of a priest who is willing to offer up his own life for others. It is this bardic nobility that shakes O'Brien's former captain from his purely martial posture.

In seminary I just pretended to be a warrior bard, and I loudly announced, "I sing a song of courage."

But at the first festal meal with the monastics, I got to *be* a bard, singing a song of courage. Then, in the most infinitesimal way, I got to be a Warrior Bard, chanting and peering into shadows for bears.

6

Breathless little mother
of everything

THROUGH DARN TOUGH SOCKS, THROUGH the rubber soles, through the aluminum deck of the *Archangel*, Fr. Andrew seems to feel the Gulf of Alaska under his toes as if barefoot beside the Lord on the Sea of Galilee. The balance of the skiff is ever so slightly off, and he asks me to take a step portside. The Suzuki four-stroke growls and whirs as it dips down into Sunny Cove. The Gulf had been swirling around the *Archangel* in her berth, but now as the propeller submerges, she moves the ocean back.

Every crossing is unrepeatable, every wave a stranger. Yet for twenty-five years the skiff has not disdained a single partner. Each wave gathers her into his arms then spins her off in a crash of merry froth down the long dance hall of Alaska's southern coast. Now she leaps high off the backhand of a swell, now slips between two rolling shoulders of the sea and traces down a cresting wave like a tear of mercury.

She rides, and from afar you may see her dipping in and out of the great blue mantle of the world, a silver needle embroidering a foam lace hem. When the seas, like the sky they mirror, "be rolled back like a scroll," on the aquamarine vellum will be traced the wake of the *Archangel*. Stitched in evanescent spume will be the many secret names of the Pacific. On the scroll will be recorded every calligraphic turn the dear boat made, glistering in the low Alaska sun, the ornate letters she looped in Monk's Lagoon, the zen-straight thrust of her keel on the beach, the entire musical score of trembling melodies that were played across her hull by the numberless pebbles as I hauled her nose onto the beach.

Once, Fr. Andrew had to take a call; he throttled way down off the beach near Monk's Rock.

"Try to keep us going in that direction," he said, stepping away from the till.

All of a sudden, I have the till. I grasp the wheel like it's a coat-rack. I brace against the shining circle like I'm holding up a man-hole cover. This is not like driving a car. It's not like driving a tractor. No, I know this feeling. My left hand is on the small of her back, my right hand is in hers. All slow dances in my life exist in a single continuum. Every time I waltz, I feel space and time collapse as every other time I've been so close to a woman floods my awareness.

For example, once again, I'm Mr. Darcy of Pemberley and Derby-shire in my senior high school play; we're in Lizzie Bennet's house, and the whole cast is trying to teach me how to waltz with her. There are explanations, words buzz around me, but I have not recovered from putting my hand on her back, feeling the crosshatched texture of her dress, the crosshatched warmth radiating against my palm and fingers. How is any man supposed to dance when he feels the indentation of a covered zipper on the lady's back?

Oh, how I repent. I should have been content to see the *Archangel* from a distance, to watch her glorious wake. But now that my hand is on her till, on the small of her back, now that she rolls under my feet and responds to my touch, I am wooden.

"I'm sorry! I'm so bad at this!"

"That's okay."

Lizzie is gracious and grim as my heart lurches drunk in my chest, gibbering:

She's alive, she's alive.

Lizzie was pretty, I knew that. But that knowledge was as nothing to this revelation—that pretty is warm, pretty has a pulse. Lizzie was not just an ideal, a *mysterium tremendum* of feminine loveliness, she was also a breathing, living creature. Everyone correctly assumed I didn't know how to waltz. But they were wrong in assuming that I knew she was alive.

Dr. Frankenstein never waltzed with Lizzie. He wouldn't have needed to make a monster if he did. If he just put his hand on her back, he'd have felt the electricity, and his heart would have cried, "She's alive! She's alive!"

Father Andrew is still on the phone.

My waltz with the waves recalls the wedding reception of my best friend from high school. The father of the bride wields a glorious handlebar mustache; he has drunk deep from the spirit in his flask and now whirls the bridesmaids like a raucous tempest, throwing them laughing in the air, catching them, and setting them down again with the savage gentleness of a satyr. The man is a hoedown unto himself, the hillbilly aspect of Bacchus—or else a singular Appalachian expression of Poseidon, far from the sea but still a rollicking series of waves beneath a flotilla of exultant bridesmaids, his arms and legs tumbling oceanic around the graceful sterns of these coiffed vessels.

They had come forth from their harbor, their dressing room, which in this highland wedding was an old slaughterhouse. The groom's party shoveled the cowpies from the aisle and dug the post holes for the wedding arch. When touring the venue, I saw, in what would be the ladies' dressing room, the circular rail affixed to the ceiling that in years past had suspended slaughtered cattle as they were butchered down the line. Now the bride is in there adorned.

Meanwhile, the bridesmaid I had accompanied down the aisle is being dipped in turn by the father of the bride in this happy dance. What a man he is.

Suddenly, he fixes me with his eye, this robust ancient mariner, and he calls out a word with all the poetic heft of Coleridge:

"Catch!"

Not even that oracular poet could have described her feet as he sets her whirling toward me. No winged bird is she, though she flies, no creature terrestrial either, though her boots strike sparks from the earth like Prometheus's own flint. Coleridge, how do I talk about the bright stitching on her boots?

In all the dark, unspeakable mystery cults of the ancient world that attempted rites of resurrection, I know they never spun a woman in a dress and cowgirl boots at a dead man. Because that would have worked; he would have come alive.

I know because I am a tin soldier in *The Nutcracker's* fourteenth army, and I came to life to catch her.

I know because I am a big and tall Macy's mannequin, and I came to life to catch her.

I know because I am Geppetto's double-jointed puppet, and I became a real boy to catch her.

I gather the motion of her in my arms. And Eve herself looks up at me through long, long lashes: the breathless little mother of everything.

It *wasn't* good to be alone. I didn't *like* it.

You could have my other ribs too, you know, if you wanted them, I think.

Aloud: "I'm sorry I'm terrible at dancing!"

And the moment is past. I have a belly button again. I am not Adam. The captain of the angels, Michael, holds the gate to Eden with a flaming sword, and I wallow in the waves in a craft named after his order. Father Andrew once mentioned that the skiff is actually named after the Archangel Gabriel. How fitting that when on the waters outside of Spruce Island or the civilized lower forty-eight states, I should find myself in a vessel named after the herald of the Annunciation. With her every splash, she whispers of a return to the Garden.

Father Andrew's phone call continues, though the glance he shoots our heading does not reassure me of my performance. I don't know how much turning of the wheel will move the rudder. Is this like a pirate ship? Should I pinwheel it dramatically? I settle for a wiggle. We crawl forward without any wake. The *Archangel* seems ponderous.

I never thought the *Archangel* was heavy until one day she went dry at extreme low tide in Sunny Cove. Herman 2 and I braced our backs up against her as the tide came in, heaving up with our legs, pushing with our shoulders. But she would not budge until the water wooed her into buoyancy once more.

A short while ago I went to my first contra dance, where a line of couples faces each other, and there's this move I was taught to spin the lady. She gives her weight to you, and you whirl her around like a censer in a church. And you have to keep that centrifugal motion going, or the charcoal will fall out of orbit and burn a hole in the carpet. The room blurs; the only thing that isn't moving is her eyes. Then you know that glory is heavy, that the spiced musk of incense requires a bold swing; else the woman doesn't trust you, and the twelve golden bells jangle to a halt.

On the dance floor, old Kepler and Copernicus are wrong: The star orbits you. Medieval people understood that only heavenly bodies could accurately describe the cosmic hugeness of even the most petite girl. It took Magellan three years and over thirty-five thousand miles to tie a bow around the earth with the wake of his ship. The circumference of Venus is thirty-two thousand miles, but I can encircle my beloved with a single arm, she whose cosmic hugeness surpasses Venus, and draw her close in a heartbeat. Oh Venus, all the cartwheels of the heavenly bodies have led to this, your side against mine, your sunflower head draped across my shoulder. When you swallow, I can hear it through my ear against your head.

The hoedown king in the men's line was wearing a pair of pants with the print of a wolf on one leg, howling at a massive full moon on the other. I have since learned that his name is Daniel, but he will forever be known to me as the Man with the Moon on His Pants. I think if he were born in another time in Norway, he would have been beloved of a Valkyrie. There being no immortal warrior maidens for solemn frolic, he poured his strength into many extra flourishes between the sanctioned moves. He clapped, flared his hips, but was ready just in time to catch the lady.

At last, Fr. Andrew's call is over, and he steps in. The throttle roars to life. I am freed from the temporal warp of the continuum of dance—only two minutes of clock time have elapsed. The skipper of St. Michael's Skete does not say a word. The hegumen of the *Archangel* adjusts the heading homeward.

The wind pulls at his beard. Beneath it may be hidden a handlebar mustache. He wears his cassock even on the boat, so we'll never know, but perhaps there's a moon on his pants.

GATSBY, GRENDEL, AND SNOWBEAR

Having lost the trail on my way back to the skete, I oriented myself by the water and struck out in what I supposed to be the right direction. There were hillocks and humps I'd never seen before, and an irrational suspicion told me that I would be lost forever. Then I saw a little merlin, each of the pale blue feathers on his wings and crest flared, hopping feebly on the forest floor. I seized upon him as the providential cause of my wandering: I was meant to save this bird. I did not want to touch him, though, diseased as he might be, so I took off my beanie, filled it with moss, then used more moss as an oven mitt and pitched the bird into the hat. I called him Gatsby.

The Great Gatsby by F. Scott Fitzgerald is one of the most divisive pieces of literature I know. Many readers are in disbelief as to how anyone can appreciate the titular protagonist. What's so great about a man who builds an illegal enterprise to woo another man's wife?

As one comedian put it, "Actually, he was just a pretty good Gatsby." I love him, though, despite everything. I put the bird I named after him in the guest cabin in a bucket, convalescing upon his couch of moss with some sugar water. Closing the door cautiously, I was careful to keep him out of the way of the cats.

On cold winter days with the water condensing on the windows, at table near the great woodburning stove, pilgrims may hear tales of the proud lineage of the cats of St. Michael's Skete. The monks each have their favorite stories of these liminal pets—how they crept onto the hallowed land of the monastery and stayed awhile to offer their creaturely gifts. Such as the dauntless Sherman, named after General William Tecumseh Sherman, who carried a whole salmon that he'd somehow caught from a stream up to a neighbor's house. Or Marmot, who could smell sadness and would visit, without fail, the monk who needed to be consoled.

These wintry stories are told in the warm skete with striking feeling. The cats are the least of God's creatures that live in that building, and their stories are the least of the memories guarded by the monks. Yet, we spoke of the cats often, as opposed to the rarity of speaking of the holy people the monks had met. To speak of the saints of God was a special occasion. When the time came to unveil such a memory, it was specific to the grace of that moment and circumstance. (Though even the cat stories are specific to the place—like the spot where Marmot lost his footing and plummeted from the monastery's battlements.)

However, I make bold to write about the cats I met during my stay at St. Michael's Skete. Something of their border-stalking nature will assist me in relocating them from the island and onto the page. So, hear now of Nora Neko and Grendel, the two cats I knew for ten months at the skete. Grendel, an old black cat with a nicked ear and chronic indigestion: I was delighted when I learned that the monks had named their cat after the wicked monster in the tenth-century Saxon epic poem *Beowulf.* In it, the noble king Hrothgar is helpless against a ravenous fiend who visits his golden hall each night and does not fail to devour at least one of his sleeping warriors. No one can prevent this until Beowulf arrives. Until then, Grendel is the terror of the hall.

And alas, our Grendel would not have hesitated to carry away Gatsby the rescued merlin. He surely had, if not his namesake's wickedness, at least a measure of his cunning. Oh Grendel, you feline king of beasts, wily veteran, silhouetted in the windowsill with a bowed head like a cowled crusader, looking down upon your domain. I miss you.

Nora was the second cat of the skete, a quarter of his age but twice his size, yet he would box her ear with his paw if his ascendancy felt challenged at the food bowl by her timid burble. Grendel was otherwise generous, allowing pilgrims extensive access to his noble person for the petting of his head, back, and belly.

Once, as I petted him, he tucked his head between his front paws and turned the most perfect somersault I ever witnessed in my life. He was in his dotage by then, taken to sprawls on the secondary trapeza table where he knew himself to be expressly forbidden. When the cook snapped at him to get down, the cat would give a pointed, languorous blink, then ease himself down. Beowulf's monster, black cat; perhaps you would be tempted to think him an old heathen, but you would be wrong.

Grendel attended chapel regularly. He sat either in the back corner by the door or beneath a *stasidi,* the characteristic monastic seats that fold open with tall arms to support a standing monk at prayer. The strangest thing was his silence. In chapel he never asked to be petted, something he insisted on at all other times. In chapel he was most himself: without irony, a lordly creature. In that sense he was like the epic poem from which he took his name. *Beowulf* is famous for being a story that predates Christianity's arrival to Britain, but the anonymous poet adds Christian elements to the old pagan tale, trying to baptize it. So there was great satisfaction in seeing this creature, named after the monster, finding its proper place in the cosmic order. As for the second cat, Nora darted into Vespers a total of three times during my stay; I called her an inquirer into the Faith.

Over two years ago, this starving calico cat appeared in misery and near death at the front door of the skete. Father Andrew set out a tin of cat food for her. While she ate, Grendel materialized from the darkness of the cat door.

"Oh no," groaned Fr. Andrew. "Leave her alone, Grendel. She's had enough."

But Grendel, though usually fiercely territorial, came up to the tin and ate with her. Father Andrew was relieved and surprised, remembering that if you could get two cats to eat from the same bowl, they would coexist peacefully. So Fr. Adrian named her *Nora Neko*, which in Japanese means "stray cat"—though Fr. Andrew privately calls her Norah Jones—and suddenly there are two cats of St. Michael's Skete.

Nora was traumatized by her past, but the fathers delicately did not ever ask her about it. They just fed her until her coat shone glossily and she began to dive for cover less often at loud sounds. When I met her, she would let me pet her but crouched low to the ground, protecting her belly, ready to bolt if I proved ungentle. She was more relaxed while we ate, stealing under the table and pressing herself against shins. We were not allowed to pet the cats during the formal meal, and this actually may have helped Nora because she got to pet us instead. She is beginning to recover from her spiritual wounds.

Things came to a head one epic day when the Grey Cat appeared. Little is known of this cat. The fathers have speculated that he is a wild cat, but well fed and strong, with a fine grey coat and a dominant stride. It is known that he sometimes scavenged for food outside the skete. Grendel, in his dotage, had not checked the interloper, and the Grey Cat grew bold. But none of us were prepared for Nora's answer to his challenge.

I will never forget it. There in my high room, still I heard the dreadful screech of combat met; this was followed by Fr. Adrian's warlike bellow as he sallied forth from his cell to lay about with his boot and separate the two combatants on the very threshold of the trapeza door. Everyone later told the story from their perspective. Father Adrian said it looked like Nora had the trespasser pinned; she was winning against the haughty cat! Monastic forensics were performed, and the only fur torn out by tooth and claw was grey.

Later, Herman 2 told me that after the fight, Nora had come to his cell and strode about it preening. Preening! A mighty, victorious warrior. This was no shrinking violet; she was come into her own now. How beautiful that cat is. Once I even heard Mother Nilia admire her perfect, little white socks. Herman 2 said that now that she had fought for us, she felt herself more confident and worthy of our love. I mentioned this theory at trapeza in front of everyone, but the normally quiet Herman 2 interrupted me.

"It's not a theory for me," he said. "I believe that."

Now I do too. She came up to my high room in the Tower—an ascent she never dared before. I was so pleased she'd come. As I pet her, she hesitated, and the normally graceful calico made a movement, unpracticed and awkward: She turned on her side. I am moved at recalling it. There was a thud as she all but fell on her flank in front of me and gave me a blessing unlooked for—a chance to pet her chest and belly. The fur was matted, because this side is never exposed, even for proper cleaning. The first time I was too eager, and she turned away. But the second chance, I just stroked her lightly with three fingers, almost holding my breath, petting Nora of the Little White Socks, brave champion of the skete.

Not all the animals recover, though. Gatsby the merlin died before lunch the same day I rescued him. In doing so he followed the path of his namesake, Jay Gatsby. It's taken a long time to figure out why I love that character so much. He's not a good man, but ever since his youth he loved a woman named Daisy. Despite his sins, he has a creaturely quality to him. The proper fulfillment of this quality allowed the fallen women of the gospel to recognize Christ and throw themselves at His mercy. This quality is the ecstatic prerogative of a person to lay all that he or she is at the feet of the beloved.

In Jay Gatsby's case it was the wrong beloved, and so he died badly—as do all who offer their souls to creature instead of Creator. Yet, in the entirety of Fitzgerald's book, Gatsby alone loves. He at least does not continually serve himself with the extravagant narcissism of America at its prime. I am certain that had he seen that the beauty that moved him about Daisy was the Lord's, he would have become a saint. Gatsby's quality of self-offering is present in animals in the way they utterly indwell their little lives.

Father Andrew sometimes watches Nora as she stalks something with her tiger stripes, ears and whiskers erect in the perfect fullness of being-what-she-is. She found her catness again at St. Michael's Skete. There is a created, animal finitude to Gatsby as well; he finds a measure of himself when he sacrifices for Daisy. The reader feels almost like a voyeur, not of his moral failings, but of his unguarded humanity. He shows us the matted fur of his belly, his longing to love and to be loved. He builds an empire on behalf of someone else. He dies pursuing her.

Saint Herman had an ox, which chose the object of its love better than Gatsby. As the saint was dying, he gave the most astonishing instruction: He told his attendants that when he died, they should "kill my ox."

Well, for some reason they didn't, and when the beast felt the departure of the saint's soul, its grief and disorientation were so vast that it ran itself into a tree and lay stunned on the ground. The villagers took pity on it and, remembering the words of the saint, cut its throat. For the ox, Herman was his saint too. The Fathers teach that the created world did not sin when its master, Adam, fell. Yet because the apex of creation fell, the rest of the created world received the consequence of death as well. After all these millennia the tragedy of that Fall still grieves us. There is an innocence to the death of animals and a sense that they only die to keep us company. They only die because we do. This happens in so many saints' lives: Their animals follow them into death.

Early this year I received a letter from one of the monks after my pilgrimage. He wrote:

I assume someone shared the sad news of Grendel's repose. About a month before he died, he suddenly went blind. He remained fairly cheerful, and he managed to make his way around the Skete without much trouble. In fact, he was able to walk down to his favorite spot in the garden everyday. Then, on the Feast of the Exaltation of the Cross, we went to the nuns for Liturgy. When we came back, no sign of Gendel. I think he chose the Nordic path and walked out into the forest when he knew his time had come. The other possibility is that he was raptured and the rest of the world remained. Anyway, he had a good full kitty life and brought entertainment to many visitors.

It's unbelievable, unsettling, the depth of feeling someone can have for an animal—as if a heart's worth of love for all the creatures of the world bursts the bonds of its repression and pours itself out for a single pet.

At a recent lecture by Dr. Martin Shaw at the Symbolic World Summit, he challenged us to make a rowan tree blush by the kind of attention we give it. As a storyteller, he surmised that everything in creation has twelve secret names, and it is our job to find those names, and in finding them, we would know the thing. One of Nora's secret names is Snowbear, and another is, possibly, Little White Socks. Herman 2 calls her Soul Kitty. She must have at least nine more names that I don't know. Next time I see Fr. Andrew, I will ask him if he has learned any of them in his observations of the little tiger, stalking in the garden.

As we continue our repentance, the consequences of the Fall are healed in small but powerful ways. Adam begins to name the beasts once more. Each name is a discovery of a quality hidden in the creature that only finds its fullness in being recognized by a human. Dr. Shaw stressed that creation wants to be admired by us. It too exists in hierarchical relationship. When we call forth these latent titles in non-human creatures, they in return teach us what it means to be created. So Adam and Eve, Lord and Lady of Creation, themselves look up to the Creator to receive their secret name from Him. The Book of Revelation says, "To him who overcomes I will give some of the hidden manna to eat. And I will give him a white stone, and on the stone a new name written which no one knows except him who receives *it*" (Rev. 2:17).

8

WINDFALL

O N SPRUCE ISLAND THE WIND blows through at great speeds; it could be a clear sunny day, but if the wind is tearing through, the *Archangel* remains in her berth. Looking out on the channel, one can read the state of the sea by the frothing teeth of the white-caps. From the Tower, through a pair of binoculars appears Monk's Rock, the incisor of Spruce Island with the tip broken off, upon which St. Herman stands in most of his iconographic depictions. The size of the blows the waves aim against the rock is the final indicator. When Monk's Rock clothes itself with a furious mantle of foam, stay home.

That rocky incisor is a microcosm of the island; it's a rock with an uneasy relationship with the other life-forms that inhabit it. The fact that it has a layer of soil on it at all is due, in large part, to the volcanic eruption of Mount Novarupta in 1912. Volcanic ash from this explosion travelled almost one hundred miles to cover the Kodiak Archipelago in ash. Whenever one digs down a few feet, one will encounter a layer of ash. It feels like a soft, light clay, and it is the inner garment of the island. The iridescent mosses are the overcoat. They warm the biosphere that over the centuries has multiplied the soil so that now, in specific spots on the island, you can keep a garden or lay a brother to rest.

Dirt is precious to the fathers of St. Michael's Skete, and assisting in the garden requires a kind of reverence for the loamy soil that the fathers have cultivated over the decades. Each year the terraces grow a little deeper as the gardeners feed the microbes and fungi with carefully turned compost, riddled with worms. They fertilize it with indigo-green seaweed that they cut from the skiff's running lines. Here, as with so many aspects of their life, they emulate St. Herman. He is the first recorded person in North America to use seaweed as fertilizer for his own garden, with which he fed the orphans in his care.

During my stay, I participated in the creation of a new bed for potatoes. We helped Fr. Andrew pound some old boards for a terrace against a depression in a slope near the garden and filled it with compost, moldy leaves, and seaweed. And between each of these layers we spread buckets of the richest mud we could gather from a secret mud source. I don't know if that bed cooked long enough to become a home for the potatoes we sowed, but I do know that the microbiology of the place will get the job done eventually.

All this to say, the garments of Spruce Island are costly, spun through the lifetimes of quintillions of microbes and fungi—and one big volcano. Thus the rootholds of the titular spruce trees are shallow. On one of my first hikes I remember our guide, Herman 1, pointing out a tree that had been uprooted in a storm. Its roots were horizontally spread out like a gnarly patchwork hand that had finally lost its grip on the ground.

"Be careful," he said. "If you step under the tree, it will snap up vertically and eat you."

But the fallen trees are not traps; they are, in the original sense of the word, windfall. In the Middle Ages, a tree could not be cut in the king's wood, and the peasants had to settle for gathering fallen branches. But when the wind knocked down an old tree, it was cause for celebration because it provided a rich harvest of wood for the whole village.

The Island is generous with her windfall—so much so that the fathers note the place where a tree fell and will let a season pass so that it dries out. The challenge comes in that most of the trees fall on slopes. That is where the most iconic work of Spruce Island begins. How many days did we, the pilgrims of St. Michael's Skete, assemble with our maul, sledgehammer, and wedges? Herman 2 has a legendary grandfather who taught him how to use a chain-saw. Wearing that grandfather's sailcloth jacket, resting the blade on his shoulder, he leads us down the slope via a deer trail.

I will never forget the first day of this work. With fragrant wood chips flying everywhere, the saw sliced the fallen trunk into rounds so large that they were impossible to carry. So, squatting down and embracing the sappy, powdered-sugar, sawdust surface, I heaved it onto its side so that I could roll it to a relatively flat spot, where I could split it with the sledgehammer.

At last all the inner monologue was silenced, all the passions stilled, as all my awareness centered on each round. Wrestling with them revealed just how inextricable are the body, soul, and mind. To be so physically aware of the wood requires all the other parts of me to align for a moment. My mind and soul are just as needed as my muscles. I am intimately aware, on a level more basic than thought, of my footfall on the moss, the quivering limits of my muscles, and my balance.

Between efforts my mind scurries around, trying to make sense of the experience through fear. What if I pitch down the slope, crushed beneath the spruce round? How similar I am to a tree, with my height and long, branch-like arms. I too would be windfall. It could happen—one of the rounds slipped from a pilgrim's hand and tumbled hundreds of feet down the ravine. It soon disappeared, but we could hear it crashing through the undergrowth. We were chastised for this by one of the fathers.

"Do you want me to go after it?" I asked.

"No. Just be careful, please," he said.

Yes, my thoughts continue at their frenetic pace, but for the first time they are not primary in my experience in the world. The great wood chunks are foremost; their awesome weight demands from me something that I didn't know I had to give: my strength. I glimpse for the first time what my voice-class teacher tried to teach me: that our bodies are not just vehicles for our magnificent brains. The monks need me to be strong for them.

I don't think I can do it. After two hours, I am gasping for breath. I feel like I have made interminable trips up the slope, and always at the bottom there is more windfall to harvest. My mouth tastes blood, and I want to sit down. It is intolerable. However, none of the other men are stopping.

I cannot break while they are not breaking. So, I continue beyond what I thought was my limit. Reality begins to change for me then, the range of my thought shrinking into a single upward step at a time. The deer path reveals itself to me then. I know which spots of moss are compacted and which are slick. I read in the torn moss the spots where I can put my boot. At the top of the slope, the stack of split rounds grows ever taller, a wall of roughly interlocking triangles of pale wood.

I blink, and it is lunchtime. We feast on quinoa bowls of kale and salmon then return to the windfall.

That day I begin to learn the way of the wedge and sledgehammer. The middle is not the best place to tap in the wedge; instead, it works best a few inches from the edge. No amount of strength can force the tool to cut through a big knot in the grain. Instead, the wedge must be placed to predict the shape of the split between two knots. The sledge does not need my help coming down; it has its weight and gravity. I am just there to lift it above my head, but not past it, so that the weight is never behind me. Then, shifting my grip so my guiding right hand slides down the haft to meet my left, I bring the hammer down.

CLANG. CRACK.

It is an instrument of only one note, so by the sound alone I know when I've struck true.

By the scent of the wood flesh,

By the give of the wood opening like a flower,

By the metallic taste in my mouth,

By the explosion of blue sparks in the dim twilight, I know I've struck true.

We work until Vespers, and I am a lighter man than I had been that morning—as if some spiritual heaviness that had been clinging to me was shaken off by the reverberation of the blows through my arms. As if contact with the earth broke through my habitual way of being and tuned me for a spell to the resonance of the island.

I feel a melancholic gladness. Sweet because I, the world-weary knower of things, did not know about this feeling, did not know that the limits I had placed on myself could be so shattered. And I am sad to have spent so much of my life sitting in chairs.

So many times while playing video games, I would be utterly engrossed by the screen, but at the end of the match there was the jarring return to the body. I found that my palms were sweaty, my mouth was open, and my posture was terrible. My gaming skill was needed, but not the rest of me. The body was just a large, awkward, unpredictable compendium of needs. But the fathers have given me this gift: They want my strength. However, each man among them is stronger than I am. My real chance to do a task that needed doing came from the nuns at St. Nilus Skete.

Oh, it was always a holiday to go to the Fifty-Five-Acre Planet. The nuns welcomed us with the greatest hospitality. They spread a fine table in the wilderness. Their home-brewed kombucha surpasses the ambrosia of the gods. However, these delicacies were a thousand times more enjoyable if we could help the nuns with some project they were working on.

It happened that summer that they needed help with their firewood supply. On the day I am thinking of, Herman 2 and I were sent to help them in the fullboat canoe. This was a special mark of independence; we did not even need Fr. Adrian to pilot us over. I knew the axes of the nuns were in poor shape, and I asked special permission to bring our maul across the water. Father Adrian sternly charged me with the responsibility for its return.

"Go keep the nuns warm!" he called as we walked out.

What a glorious mission. I even wrapped the head of the maul with a towel so that it did not puncture the side of the fullboat.

So that morning Herman and I traipsed down to the beach, awash with brine and focus. There was a chainsaw on the nuns' island already for him, so we carried our canoe down the shore and stowed the maul inside. We paddled over the flat, calm water in a jiffy.

The mother superior of the island greeted us herself and began to direct us to windfalls to process. There were piles of rounds all over the island. She set me splitting on one of them and promised to come back and show me the next in a bit.

I was determined to have the pile split before she returned. I was more focused than I ever remember being in my life. There is so much grace on that island that it tuned my efforts. Really, that much trying usually gets in the way of efficiency because the over-abundance of effort lends itself to rigidity.

I knew I had to pace myself, so I lifted the maul just high enough to get the split, calculating by the width of the round. There was no strength to spare for a display; if I hit the wood too hard, I'd spend extra precious seconds chasing the two halves that went flying into the undergrowth. I slipped into the flow—every step was perfect, none of my movements wasted. So when the mother superior returned, she was awesomely taken aback.

"When you've finished—oh, you're already done!"

This sentence lives in a place of honor in my memory as one of the loveliest I have ever heard.

You're already done.

We ate lunch with the nuns that day, and after the reading at table, I must confess that I rather held forth to them. There were no fathers present, and Herman is usually quiet at such gatherings. So I drank deeply of the kombucha and talked a great deal. The only better feeling in the world than making the monks laugh is making the nuns laugh. It's a merry, high-stakes art.

That afternoon we continued working, and one of the sisters came up with a tray of monastic brownies. Something has happened with them, she explained, and they are extremely gooey. I tell you, they were the best brownies in the entire world, scooped hot out of the pan by two ravenous woodmen. I have worked much with my hands since, but that day is the gold standard of workflow and grace. Would that I could move again like the man I was that day.

Vespers had already begun at our own skete when we finished that evening. This gave us a good reason to brave the crossing in our canoe rather than call for a pickup in the skiff. The waves were much more pronounced, however. On the beach, once we said good-bye and when there were no nuns watching, Herman and I began to hype each other up for the journey. We were both exhausted, and my upper body was spent from all the times I raised my maul high.

So, we needed a last burst of excitement to send us across. I sat at my place in the front because you should always put your big gun in the back. Herman took that spot, and as the waves lapped around us, we began to paddle furiously.

After almost thirty seconds of maximum exertion, Herman and I looked around at the same time to realize we were still sitting on the beach! The waves flowing around us deceived us. We had not actually pushed off, and now all our hype was wasted.

We're gonna die, I thought, and we both busted up laughing.

Still, we could not call the fathers. Our beach was right there. We just had to row a third of a mile. This time we make it off the beach, and almost immediately, muscles that I didn't know existed burn in my trapezoids and shoulders. The fire is exquisite torture.

As our little coracle bobs and splashes on the waves a quarter of the way there, I have to take a break.

"I'm sorry, Herman!" I yell as I rest my oar for a second on the boat. But he is strong enough for both of us, and without a word—perhaps with the help of his saint—continues his strong, steady stroke. I join after a moment, but it is he who gets us home.

I tell the story of that crossing whenever I am talking about St. Innocent of Alaska. If it was that hard for us to make it a stone's throw away to the opposite beach, how did St. Innocent traverse thousands of miles in his *baidarka,* a traditional Aleutian super lightweight canoe made of animal skins stretched over a wooden frame? He too was a tall man and had to kneel for countless hours in that tiny vessel. The rider's parka had to be sewn into the canoe to keep it watertight. The saints were men of mighty strength. Since childhood, I have embedded in my mind's eye the image of St. Herman lifting an enormous log on his shoulders and carrying it barefoot to the place it was needed. The witnesses say it would have taken four men to move such a log. I don't think we only lack the strength—their whole way of being was different.

The closest corollary I have of this special strength was during my seminary years when I visited the Bulgarian Orthodox Monastery of St. John the Baptist in Warwick, Massachusetts. Their bishop was also their abbot, and, after presiding over the services, he led the work team in digging a deep trench across the road. We were three young seminarians, but we could not keep up with the vigor of the middle-aged bishop. With his cassock knotted to free up his legs, his pickax struck like lightning! He did the hardest work, breaking up the ground ahead of us so that it would be easier for us to dig. Three young men were not worth one of him. It was so glorious—totally Arthurian in that the leader was not just the wisest, but undoubtedly the strongest. How I rejoiced when I learned he was elected the patriarch of Bulgaria.

At the end of their lives, these spiritual giants themselves become windfall, fully ripe in virtue and grace until they are harvested by God. Their repose leaves a lasting sanctification on the land. The flame of St. Nilus's presence, alive in Christ, quickens the nuns of the skete named after him more than the woodburning stove. Saint Herman's intercessions have protected the fathers of Spruce Island more times than we can know.

9

EVERY TREE A LANCE

WHILE ON SPRUCE ISLAND, I traversed the world without a smartphone. I entrusted mine to Fr. Andrew and only asked for it every few weeks to attend to some matter. It took me almost a month to acclimate to the anxiety of not having its comforting weight in my pocket, to ignore a version of that panic we get when slapping the outside of our jeans and finding nothing there. It felt like a missing appendage; the only scrolling I had constant access to were the thirty-three knots of a prayer rope. This did not provide the same mesmeric comfort. It was a more difficult consolation.

I also did not have access to recorded music. It is so easy. It soothes with an artificially unchanging soundscape: each beat identically the same; every inflection, every mistake, the mix of the sound; its virtue in its sameness. Since my teenage years, my habit has been to devour the same track thousands of times across decades until the score and lyrics become attuned to the very resonance of my being. Those three minutes are a pristine ideal—a frozen, looping, perfect sound world. Being without my phone on Spruce Island, I realized how dependent I had been on that world for comfort.

I felt I needed this consolation because at some point in childhood's end, I had lost my sense of being sustained by God's grace. If His grace is water, I started to feel that I could no longer float in it but needed to thrash, kick, and swim just to stay alive. Life became a riddle to be solved, not a mystery to be lived. The books that began to appeal to me were dystopian young adult novels in which all other concerns are secondary to the main imperative: Stay alive.

The message of these books became a kind of refrain. What do I need to do in this instance to stay alive? What am I missing that might kill me? What factor is present that will morph into a threat?

This survival attitude was glaringly at odds with Spruce Island in the summer. If the island has a riddle, it does not seem to accord it much notice. It is too busy decking itself out as if for a ball. It wears countless strings of rubies—the sweet salmon berries. It wraps itself in a brown velvet cape of mushrooms. The laughing creek pours itself like a crystal sash over the island's shoulder. The abundant black currants and huckleberries cluster like earrings.

This is no perfect, carefully recorded, unchanging soundscape. The whole island has a romping, jovial quality, each life-form tripping over itself on its way to the Source of its being. Nothing is perfect here; everything is quick, teeming with micro- and macroscopic life. All of it stretches toward the low-arcing sun, growing every hour a little closer. And each day the sun throws different rays from different angles so that the most familiar tree shows up a glorious stranger in solar-filigreed lichen, hemmed in a lace of Spanish moss twined with sunbeams. The longest day contains eighteen hours of light on Spruce Island, so the strangeness is amplified by the very fact that it is so unhurried. Trees had to be created as rooted things; their upward motion is terrible enough. If they moved laterally, then the axis of the world would constantly shift. My point is that trees already move enough. They are not as stationary as my songs; they have the audacity to change.

This is a wild place. There is no way to control any of these myriad variables. How could I frame a square-shaped riddle on these curving boughs? So, not being able to fit the forest in a category, it became a source of some anxiety for me. I do not have the courage to listen to the silence of its sylvan transepts or the speech of its many creatures. The gothic cathedrals of Spain made me feel pleasantly tiny, but their stone pillars don't grow after the vault is set on them. In the woods I stride through the pillars of the cathedral of the sky, contending with the momentum of the trees, their explosive longing expressed in every reaching needle. I can't deal with it, the questing forest's headlong tilt toward the Holy Grail. Trees are all lance. Peaceful? Ha. The only man who could be at peace here is one whose upward drive for Christ was greater than the forest's. His name was St. Herman Ivanovich Popov.

This is the central agony of living on Spruce Island. On one hand, my deep heart rejoices at the call to adventure, each pine finger pointing toward the direction my soul has tended since it was created in my mother's womb. On the other hand, I want to be safe. I had reached Paradise's own threshold; could I not be allowed to huddle in the doorway? My deep heart feels a kinship with its fellow tall beings, the trees. But the survivor, once I had enough firewood, just wanted them to point less insistently toward Christ.

I dodge around the paths, stepping carefully over roots, singing pop songs by myself just to hear the familiar chord progressions. Often I bring a hiking pole with me, and the spike at the end of it serves as a third anchor point to the path. There is an invisible spike as well, the anchoring song. Still, even within those songs is the same seed of wildlife as the forest.

In patristic thought the soul is always characterized as feminine. It is the Bride that is mystically married to Christ; she longs for the heavenly Bridegroom. The psalmist speaks to this aspect of us in a verse we hear during the paraklesis to the Theotokos:

Listen, O Daughter, and see, and incline your ear, and forget your people and your father's house, and the King will desire your beauty.[16]

By receiving the dignity of being wedded to the King, the soul is made royal. It is *The Princess Bride*.

Oh yes.

I quoted that film extensively on a hike up Mount St. Herman. Out of nowhere, a fellow pilgrim who was usually quiet spoke up and said, "I think you quote movies so much because they make you feel safe."

Where did he get off being so observant? Yes, the survivor in me loves the familiarity of movie quotes. How could I not think of the masked Man in Black's battle of wits with Vizzini as I walked through the mythic terrain of the mountain?

Each frame of that scene is a painting hung in a gallery of my memory. How Vizzini, the ultimate riddle solver, the ultimate

---

16   Nicholas Kasemeotis, ed., trans. Demetri Kangelaris and Nicholas Kase-meotes, *The Service of the Small Paraklesis to the Most Holy Theotokos* (Holy Cross Orthodox Press, 1984), 18.

mind—one of such potency that Plato, Socrates, and Aristotle were "morons" by comparison—held a knife to Princess Buttercup's throat. Right there, the cunning mind held the soul hostage from her True Love. So, the mysterious Man in Black, the Dread Pirate Roberts, Westley the Beloved, offers his famous challenge:

> "You're that smart, huh? In that case I challenge you to a battle of wits."
> "For the princess?" asked Vizzini.
> A nod.
> "To the death?"
> Another nod.
> "Very well, I accept."[17]

The struggle is always thus: for the princess, to the death. At last I know what the existential stakes of that duel were: the freedom of the soul from the tyranny of the mind. They may as well have been seated on the shale stones of Mount St. Herman!

The wine is poured, and Westley hides both cups behind him. After placing them again before each man, he explains that he has poisoned one cup. Vizzini must choose which cup to drink from.

The mastermind plays the game just as I would; he thinks he can deduce the position of the poison based on all the information he has about his opponent. Except that he has not understood the most important aspect of his enemy. Namely, Westley is driven by a force that both undergirds all reality and exists above it: True Love. In the book, William Goldman reveals that at every impossible challenge Westley never, even for an instant, considers the possibility of failure. He is pure action for the rescue of Buttercup,

---

17   *The Princess Bride*, directed by Rob Reiner (20th Century Studios, 1987).

beyond determination, beyond the rational, beyond the limits of the possible.

In the end it is Vizzini, the superior intellect, who falls dead. Both goblets were poisoned, but Westley had spent the previous five years building up an immunity to the toxin. It is as if the created world itself is a friend to the Beloved and refuses to harm him.

Of course, Buttercup does not immediately recognize him because of his dark disguise. However, after she pushes him down a steep ravine, he calls to her, revealing his identity. So the Princess Bride, with utter abandon, throws herself after him, disdaining all dangers.

As she tumbles head over heels, she is at one with the created world that also chases True Love. Like the toxin that does not harm Westley, neither is she hurt by the steep fall. She is at last moving toward the Beloved, and so her fall is aligned with the motion of all the universe, which also chases the Beloved. And I begin to understand life is not a riddle but a Person with whom all creation is acquainted and to whom all creation is returning.

With Vizzini in mind, I perceive the up-thrusting trees as so many lances whose trajectory I can never map. As such, they are only threats to be managed. Their magnificence causes me to scratch my head and cogitate. I've spent hours trying to figure them out. Yet I too was missing a crucial variable because trees also have souls.

As St. Dionysios the Areopagite and St. Maximos the Confessor teach, God creates each thing by revealing to nonbeing a facet of His Beauty. Christ is so beautiful in this particular facet of His Uncreated Energies that a tree is wooed from nonexistence into being. Its very fidelity to being a tree is a response to Christ's Beauty. The unchanging nature of creation is a testament to its devotion to Christ; the way creation loves God is by being itself. Herman 2 connected me with one of his dearest friends, the poet J. Z. Schafer, who constantly explores this theme in his work. When working on this chapter, using his poetic charism, Schafer explained it to me this way:[18]

When nonbeing saw the Spirit hovering over the face of the waters, it fell in love; it forgot about itself; it moved toward the beloved.

The world was created, as the Gospels tell us, through the Logos, the son of God, and thus the world bears His mark, His shape; and that shape is cruciform, an everlasting valentine written directly to us.

There are daisies because the breath of Christ is fragrant as a daisy; there are thunderstorms because His voice is like a thundering; there are lions because His glory radiates in spokes of golden fire; there are trees of oak because Christ is strong and ancient.

Saint Maximus tells us that the Logos was incarnate three times: first, in the world itself; second, in the Scriptures; and finally, in taking on and uniting Himself completely to our human nature.

Created things are, in essence, nothing. Christ shares his Life with everything; He gives life, for His is the only true Life. Things exist only when they are gazing upon His face; and when they turn away (as only humans are wont to do) they fade into themselves, wraiths who can never quite reject the honeyed gift of *ruach*, of breath. The stability that one can observe in the forms of nature—the fact that beings do not shapeshift ceaselessly before our eyes, adrift in the flux of elfin, quantum riptides—exists because every being is anchored to the vision of Christ and drawing closer and closer to Him, until He is all

---

18   He graciously gave permission for me to use his words.

in all. People, however, must repeat in themselves that cruciform gesture of self-forgetfulness, cease looking at how their shadows pool around themselves upon the ground, and gaze like eagles on the entelechial Sun in order to exist at all. We are chicks gathered beneath their mother's wing.

Thus creation itself mourns and cries out against the death of its Creator during the Passion of the Lord. Rocks cannot hold together in the face of the Reason for Existence being put to death. They burst asunder. The sun cannot perform his duties but hides his golden face. The earth cannot maintain her composure but shakes. These details are not poetic embellishments by the evangelists but the reaction of a cosmos in relationship to the God who dies and resurrects.

And it is a tree that is the most faithful to God in that hour. While at the skete, I read an excerpt from "The Dream of the Rood," an Anglo-Saxon poem from the eighth century in which a pious poet tells of a vision in which he heard the Lord's Cross speak. The wood trembled to see the Lord approaching to be crucified upon it:

Twas long ago (I remember it still)
That I was hewn at end of a grove,
Stripped from off my stem; strong foes laid hold of me there,
Wrought for themselves a show, bade felons raise me up;
Men bore me on their shoulders, till on a mount they set me;
Fiends many fixed me there. Then saw I mankind's Lord
Hasten with mickle might, for He would sty upon me.
There durst I not 'gainst word of the Lord
Bow down or break, when saw I tremble
The surface of earth; I might then all

My foes have felled, yet fast I stood.
The Hero young begirt Himself, Almighty God was He,
Strong and stern of mind; He stied on the gallows high,
Bold in sight of many, for man He would redeem.
I shook when the Hero clasped me, yet durst not bow to earth,
Fall to surface of earth, but firm I must there stand.
A rood was I upreared; I raised the mighty King,
The Lord of Heaven; I durst not bend me.[19]

The tree did not split; it held Him up, cooperating with the Savior's mission. This poet indeed gives language to the tree and thought. However, that is a literary tool to suggest the rootedness of the tree's being in Christ. Thought is not required for Creation to choose Christ; it chooses Him the way a baby chooses her mother's breast.

All along I was not dealing with Spruce Island on its own terms. I felt as C. S. Lewis writes in the *The Weight of Glory*,

We have been mere spectators. Beauty has smiled, but not to welcome us; her face was turned in our direction, but not to see us. We have not been accepted, welcomed, or taken into the dance. We may go when we please, we may stay if we can: "Nobody marks us."[20]

Turned toward the forest, I am frustrated and bewildered, not realizing the island is looking over my shoulder, beholding Christ.

---

19 James M. Garnett, *Elene; Judith; Athelstan, or The Fight at Brunanburh; Byrhtnoth, or The Fight at Maldon; and The Dream of the Rood* (Ginn & Company, 1902), 72–73.

20 C. S. Lewis, *The Weight of Glory and Other Addresses* (The Macmillan Company, 1949), 11.

Without acknowledging and sharing this vision of the Beautiful, how could I know the forest on the level of its most essential being? I could not see it properly because I did not realize that it too is beholding. I was trying to dance with someone who already had a partner. It was like being caught before a great thicket of lowered lances, tilting toward their target with inevitable, glacial speed. So, the only way to see the island truly is to fix my gaze on the Beloved and see it in my peripheral vision. This glimpse from the corner of my eye is truer than accosting it from the front.

My singing and movie quotes never felt wrong in the woods. The notes of creaturely longing ring true in a forest of creatures longing for Christ. There in the sylvan cathedral, the fallen aspects of the culture hold no sway. The fallen aspects of art, darkened by the passions, are muted by the shining of the holy parts.

The mistake is to use the culture as a shield or anchor. Instead, the stories, music, and quotes all point to a glorious tumble through undergrowth, a besting of giants, Spaniards, and geniuses—Princess Buttercup riding a white horse at the side of her Beloved.

My favorite poem thus far by J. Z. Schafer is this one:[21]

He wept into his hands.
I have not time enough, he said,
To read these thousand books;
An owl on a thin branch replied, and those who wrote,
What did they look upon in writing them?
He mused and said, they looked upon
A dark-eyed beautiful lady
With elderberries in her breast,
Upon a yellow coracle

---

21 Unpublished. Printed with permission from the author.

The moon's high tide abreast;
They looked upon the leaves old age
Had goldened for their rest;
They looked upon the battlefield
Either in bloody field or in the breast.
And what is it that they were looking for?
For God who is in all of these, I wit.

10

₭NEELING BEFORE THE KING

ON A FEAST DAY, ST. Michael's Skete becomes a mead hall. From the far corners of each cell the fathers and brothers gather, the nuns join them from their island, and their neighbors in the borough crowd into the chapel of the Archangel Michael. The desert wanderers of the fast are at last gathered together. After the hours spent in prayer in their cells, after the absence from needless speech, and the long, hungry hours alone, the strugglers are changed. In imperceptible ways they have a blessed strangeness about them so that the Liturgy and the feast that follows have the dignity of a meeting of strangers and the familiarity of old friends. All are united in palpable joy: We made it!

Like Arthurian knights or thanes of a mighty chieftain, the gifts of each member of the community rise to the surface in the struggle and shine in the feast. There is the monk who leads the chanting and who has taught the brothers old, pious Christmas carols so that we "don't embarrass ourselves in front of the nuns." There is the monk who tirelessly maintains the fire in the central stove to keep the place warm. Seated beside me is the brother who bakes all the breads. Across from me is a brother who weaves prayer ropes and works handicrafts. Of course, in a monastic community these gifts are not praised with titles. It is only after someone is safe from vanity and glorified as a saint that they are given titles such as St. George the Trophybearer and St. Romanos the Melodist. The saints have no risk of mistaking true Glory for their own, just as the father superior strives to lead with his own will utterly aligned to Christ's will.

There at the head of the table is the chair of the hegumen. It is the only chair in the skete that has arms and a back, and it is further ennobled by faded burgundy upholstery. The finish of the wood has paled at the curling edge of the arms where the lacquer has been worn away by the forearms of the hegumenoi of St. Michael's Skete. The fathers sit on the benches closest to Fr. Andrew, who is that rustic throne's current occupant, then the brothers from the most senior, and then the pilgrims, visitors, and neighbors—order on earth as it is in heaven.[22]

Though the office of hegumen is quite distinct from a king's, the way Fr. Andrew presided over our merriment had a regal quality. He was the Big Man; he answered for us and for the life of the little monastery. If blood or shame were demanded of the brotherhood, it would be his blood, and he would bear the shame. He was, in truth, Father. He bore the burden of hearing the confessions of all the monks, brethren, pilgrims, and neighbors. I believe the greatest blessing a confessor gives is not his counsel during confession but the unclouded eye he turns upon you the next morning. He

---

22 The honorific of "father" is given to those monks of rassophore rank and higher. The honorific of "brother" is for novices and sometimes longtime pilgrims with fraternal bonds.

gave us the gifts of his unaltered good humor and his steady gaze. It is an echo of God's unchanging regard for us, despite the sins we have committed.

The gaze of the king at once honors the image of God in us and makes intolerable the sins that occlude it. Recall in Mark 10:21, "And *Jesus looking upon him loved him, and said to him,* 'You lack one thing; go, sell what you have, and give to the poor, and you will have treasure in heaven; and come, follow me'" (RSV, emphasis mine). Every one of us has a deep soul need to be looked upon and loved by the King. Dr. Martin Shaw, that wonderful mythologist, calls it "the confirming glance of the king." We long to perform self-emptying quests beneath such eyes. How well I remember a certain workday a brother and I were carrying two-by-six boards up the final ascent of the hill from a neighbor's house to the work site at the skete. I relished the challenge of balancing the long heavy boards on my shoulder and marching them up the hill determined as an ant. However, before the last of the boards were moved the brother working with me felt ill and had to stop. Not giving me a chance to feel resentful or superior to this brother, Fr. Andrew himself took the brother's place. Seeing the older man's focus and the effort it cost him to climb the hill weighed down by boards, my own fatigue evaporated. I was filled with fire; I all but fled up and down the hill, pursued by the image of his gallantry. There were no more risks; if my heart burst, I should have been glad to die in such company. However, not all quests I volunteered for were so noble.

I remember near the end of one feast I heard about the illegal hunting of octopi. The topic came up after dessert, which is heralded by the bright twinkle of a bell next to Fr. Andrew's plate. The cook would rise and bring the cake out to Fr. Andrew, presenting it to him along with a knife. On a Sunday, there would be a murmur of appreciation for the confection, and Fr. Andrew would make the sign of the cross on the frosting with the knife. This last blessing and decoration complete, the cook returned to the kitchen to carefully divide this treasure among us. It was my self-appointed role to carry the little plates out as he set the dessert upon them.

It was then that one of the neighbors mentioned how some folks were hunting illegally for octopi by pouring bleach into the shallow water near the crevices where the creatures lived. I had not known there were octopi on our island and immediately burst in, "Father, bless me to hunt for octopus."

Father blinked and said that I might.

My speech had as much to do with desire for the hunt as it did to say something before the assembly in the feasting hall. I declared to everyone that I would not use these foul bleach-water methods of catching the subterranean delicacies. Instead, I would use the old way, and, even as I spoke, my courage faltered a bit. The old way involves sticking one's arm into the crevices as bait and pulling the cephalopod out when it tries to pull me in. Still, visions of returning with a bucket full of octopi, my arm puckered with glorious red welts from the combat, cheered me.

I consulted the tide book and found a morning two weeks later when there would be extreme low tide. This is a remarkable sight because the underbelly of the sea is exposed, the skiff is beached on her running lines, and one can walk to spots in the coves that are almost always submerged. The undersides of the rocks and promontories are coated with a slimy layer of barnacles, dank seaweed, starfish, and water moss. Next came the part that still seems surreal to me. I velcroed up the left sleeve of my waterproof jacket. My naked arm in the overcast day never seemed so wondrous and so beautiful. Oh, its cleverness—the movement of the tendons and the vivifying blue traceries of the veins beneath the skin. It seemed far too wonderful a thing to be used as bait in the subterranean slime.

How to describe this descent? My heart pounded with two rival hopes: that a tentacle would grab my hand, and that a tentacle would not grab my hand. That my five fingers would meet the eight arms and that they would encounter nothing but algae and barnacles. To my relief, the crevice was empty. I went farther out, to rocks one could only walk to once or twice a month. There in my waterproof armor, I laid down on the flat part of the promontory. My body pressed against the wet stone, my arm buried up to my shoulder in the inky green depths.

I toiled all morning but caught nothing. This had been a fruitless, self-willed quest. An adventure has to be given—only then does the mythic beast, the little kraken, appear. As in the following tale, which is often told with delight at table during a feast.

They say and say truly that once, a group of Protestants was attempting to retrieve their halibut line in the company of their guide, a local Orthodox deacon. To their dismay, the buoy came loose, and they lost the line. The halibut line rests about a foot off the seafloor, so the only thing they could do was dredge for it. All they had was a hammer, so they tied a hammer to a line, threw it overboard, and dragged the area they had lost the buoy, hoping to catch their own line. Well, after a long time of fruitless dragging, the situation was becoming desperate; they were not even sure they were in the right place. At this point, the good deacon decides he needs to pray to St. Theophilus, the fool for Christ. He announces his intent to the Protestants and does three prostrations to the saint on the deck of the boat. A moment later, the dredge line snags on something. Excited, they haul up the hammer, and, lo and behold: Holding the hammer in one tentacle and the halibut line in the other is a mighty octopus! The saint had sent an octopus to make the connection. They returned it to the deep in gratitude.

Before Fr. Andrew blessed a quest, he considered each brother and how the mission would affect him. His instructions and sermons were alike in this careful balancing of strengths. There were so few of us that we formed the loom for the weave of the tapestry of his speech. His sermons did not just cover each of us, but the space between us. An outsider heard a simple gospel message, but the way he wove his themes addressed all the positive and negative tensions in our community.

Each week with bowed head, we whispered our confession to him and to Christ, telling of all the times we had betrayed the King. At the end, we knelt, neck exposed for a sword blow that never came. Instead, Fr. Andrew covered my head and neck with his stole and read the prayer of forgiveness. Once, in confession, I mentioned that I was not at that moment wearing a cross. Father Andrew stopped me, went to the drawer in the vestry, and drew out a simple wooden cross—a match to his own—and put it on me. That cross will only leave my neck when I die.

I would not have come to love the Arthurian legends without my stay at Fr. Andrew's table. I understand better how the knights conducted themselves, encouraging one another to glorious feats such as catching octopi because the glory of one blessed the whole table. And all for love of King Arthur, on his lonely seat of faded burgundy.

We look up to our leaders, but there are precious few men who can look down on and affirm them. They constantly give a gift of beholding that they may need to wait to the end of their lives to receive from another. Saint Paul waited also; he longed to leave this life to hear the words spoken over his bowed head, "Well done, good and faithful servant."

Father Andrew will bow to no other king than Christ. Perhaps the most vivid memory I have of him was at the funeral of his old friend. The monks were asked to dig the grave, as the friend wanted his final resting place to be on Spruce Island. We did so with difficulty because there were few places on the old man's property where the soil was six feet deep. When we lowered the coffin, a family member asked Fr. Andrew to pray. Just as he was blessing the name of the Holy Trinity, a man from a different family branch interrupted.

"Actually, we are Jehovah's Witnesses, and so *I* will say the prayer."

I was shocked and outraged. How dare he interrupt the hegumen with his heresies? But Fr. Andrew gave way without a word. Despite my ire, through sheer force of habit, when the man started to pray, I bowed my head.

"Jehovah God," the man began. Then I thought, *Wait a second—I don't pray to this non-Trinitarian God. I can't pray with JWs.*

I looked up. Every head in the gathering was bowed, bending like stalks of ripe grain, save one. My beloved hegumen looked out toward the horizon with head unbowed.

11

J. R. R. TOLKIEN AND THE
ROMANOV ROYAL MARTYRS

THE FATHERS PLANTED A CANADIAN maple by the path down
to the terraced garden, and it is visible through the kitchen
window. It is one of the only trees of Spruce Island that changes
colors in the fall, a painfully short season on this evergreen land.
Once, a storm blew through in late September and took off all the
leaves prematurely, killing autumn early and leaving Fr. Andrew
depressed. But during that season when I was on my long pilgrimage, I remember a perfect autumn day while coming up from the
Cove with him. He had parked the four-wheeler, and I was helping
carry a tote down the path to the east entrance of the skete.

At the entrance to this short path, affixed to a tree in a wooden
frame with a tiny roof, is an enamel icon of Michael the Archangel,
guarding the border of the property. We venerated this icon as we
always do on our return, then continued down this straight path
along a ridge of the hill. It looks out on the Cove on the southwest

side and up to the main chapel of the skete on the other. It is the final approach to the skete, a surprisingly flat way compacted by countless footfalls. It is a space to collect yourself a little, tuck in your shirt, and catch your breath after the huff up the hill.

That day the sun was setting, hitting the path with a special perfection. Father Andrew likes to say that mornings belong to St. Nilus Island but afternoons to Spruce. Never was that statement truer as we walked the little path. The forest seemed specially designed to hold the westering sunlight in its branches, its trillion spruce needles fine enough to grasp the gossamer strands of photons. The sun luxuriated especially in the red leaves of the maple, causing it to blaze like the skete's own torch. A feeling of blessedness welled up in me at the sight, which reached a joyous crescendo when Fr. Andrew said, "It looks like Rivendell."

Then, one of the venerable men staying at the skete emerged onto the path to the garden, and I cried, "It's Elrond!"

Alas, woe is me! For this excellent man hated Tolkien's work more than anyone I have ever met. It had been a point of contention between us already, and my comment immediately provoked a surprisingly bitter argument. Finally, trying to make peace with me, he suggested a deal.

"How about this? I won't criticize Tolkien if you don't quote him."

"I appreciate your diplomacy," I said. "I'm sorry, but I can't agree. Sometimes I have to quote him."

So we worked around each other on this point of tension, because his disdain for the legendarium bothered me almost as much as my continual references bothered him. His position troubled me because he otherwise had a fantastic literary palate. He challenged my previous assumption that everyone who hated Tolkien was either mad and cynical or bereft of all good taste. Now, I believe that most haters secretly feel betrayed and disoriented by experiencing such heraldic glory in an imaginal world. What right does Tolkien have to move us so within a realm of hairy-footed hobbits, tree herders, and elves? They resent beauty being in a place they believe they cannot access, avenging themselves on it by calling it childish escapism. With a grim courage they pass over the *The Hobbit* and pick up the newspaper. Within its black-and-white pages they find a suffering world that seems entirely unalleviated by adventures in Middle-earth. However, those worlds collided for me during a solo trip to Monk's Lagoon.

It happened that I received a blessing to spend a couple nights in the skid cabin there. I did not want to take my mobile phone with me to disrupt my solitude, but Fr. Andrew did not feel comfortable with my having no way to call for help if I fell into a hole or one of the two man-eating bogs in the forest. He solved this problem by digging out the skete's old VHF radio set. They were basically marine walkie-talkies. Now I could converse with HQ via the local radio waves.

"You're going to need a handle," he said. "But it can't be silly, because we'll be on a public channel."

Of course, I was thrilled at this opportunity for naming but couldn't think of a good one. After a moment Fr. Andrew said, "How about 'Shire Mobile'?"

I instantly loved it and use it to this day on the radio channel of the farm where I work.

As I hiked to Monk's Lagoon with my forty-liter waterproof backpack stocked full of provisions, I tested the range of the radio.

"This is Shire Mobile calling New Valaam. I repeat, this is Shire Mobile calling New Valaam. Over."

After a moment Fr. Andrew acknowledged, and I said, "We've got clear skies. The sun is shining, and the road goes ever on."

"Copy that, Shire Mobile. And on and on," came the sign-off from New Valaam.

I reached Monk's Lagoon without a problem, and my impression was just as numinous as my first stay.[23]

It's always an especial blessing and pleasure to work up a thirst on the hike only to drink my fill at St. Herman's miracle-working spring by the church. After drinking and venerating a little, I returned to the spring with empty gallon bottles from the cabin so that I could cook and drink blessed water my entire stay. There is such a rightness to holy water not being limited to a small plastic vial brought home from the service of Theophany. Christ sanctified all the waters of the earth when he was baptized in the Jordan, and St. Herman's holiness provided a conduit for that sanctifying moment to be presented anew to the little spring.

I wanted to say prayers in each of the three chapels. I stopped first in the largest church of St. Sergius and St. Herman of Valaam and then the Kaluga Chapel. After that, I got cozy lighting the stove and cooking a simple dinner on it. It was dark by then, and I had saved the chapel closest to the cabin for last. I took a candle, lighter, and the *Akathist to the Tsar Martyr Nicholas II*.

You see, in addition to the three icons of the Mother of God I mentioned in the introduction, there is another icon that I saw every day when I descended the Tower. It faced me down the hall. In it are depicted the Romanov martyrs in their glory as saints of the Church. It was not until their feast day, though, that I began to venerate and pray to them.

I confess: Despite not knowing their story, I was skeptical of political figures being canonized. It seemed to me that there is always a chance of ulterior motives for glorifying powerful historical men and women, though the greatest aspect of their story that kept me away was the tragedy of their murder by the Bolsheviks.

---

23   See Chapter 1, "Enter the Castle."

I did not want to love people only to have to join the rest of those who loved them in mourning for their deaths. I did not want to feel their absence.

I didn't have a choice, though. I should have known that if the Romanovs were in that corridor leading to my tower, they would end up entering my life eventually. As I have said, that skete seemed to be the place where time collapsed in on itself, including the future. The fathers of St. Michael's Skete keep the feast day of the Royal Martyrs with special love, and for the lunchtime reading Fr. Andrew picked an especially moving passage quoted in the definitive account of their lives, *The Romanov Royal Martyrs: What Silence Could Not Conceal*. The passage referenced an eyewitness to Tsaritsa Alexandra's nursing of the wounded during World War 1:

> From that time on our days were literally devoted to toil. We rose at seven in the morning and very often it was an hour or two after midnight before we sought our beds. . . . The Empress literally shirked nothing. Sometimes when an unfortunate soldier was told by the surgeons that he must suffer an amputation or undergo an operation which might be fatal, he turned in his bed calling out her name in anguished appeal. "Tsaritsa! Stand near me. Hold my hand that I may have courage." Were the man an officer or a simple peasant boy she always answered the appeal. With her arm under his head she would speak words of comfort and encouragement, praying with him while preparations for the operation were in progress, her own hands assisting in the merciful work of anesthesia. The men idolized her, watched for her coming, reached out bandaged hands to touch her as she passed, smiling happily as she bent over their pillows. Even the dying

smiled as she knelt beside their beds murmuring last words of prayer and consolation.[24]

That riveted my attention—this, a grace queenlier than any fantasy novel. As soon as possible I spirited the book up to the Tower and set Tolkien aside to read it. The experience of reading the account of the Romanovs' lives and death surpassed any other time I've read either hagiography or biography, though this book belongs to both genres. The text blazed with uncreated fire but was not consumed. I do not have space or quotations enough to prove it to you, but with all my authority as a high school English teacher and consummate bibliophile, I say I have read a thousand, thousand books to get to that one.

A portrait emerges of the royal family of such resounding trueness that it sends the bell of authenticity clanging in my heart. Shockingly, this is the same bell that rang during some passages of Tolkien. How could this be? There in the Tower, I began to ponder that by the workings of the Logos outside of time, and by weaving even imaginal worlds into His tapestry, the kenotic glory of Middle-earth's fictional characters finds its fulfillment in the self-emptying of the Romanov family at the end of World War I.

If the secondary, imaginal world is True and Beautiful, it accesses those aspects of Christ in a way that presents no competition between imagination and history. The hierarchy resolves the confusion: The Romanovs are like Christ, and Tolkien's characters are like the Romanovs. Literature, then, is a bright stitching on the hem of the martyrs' glorious robes. In an infinitely high and

---

24 Anna Viroubova, *Memories of the Russian Court* (Macmillan and Co., Limited, 1923), 110.

personal way, the martyrs become the adornment of the body of Christ. And for imaginative literature to have real power, it must participate in the cosmos somehow. And it does, as a filagree on the tsar's epaulettes.

The lives of J. R. R. Tolkien and Tsar Nicholas II are connected by their sacrificial service in the first World War. Many scholars and fans have tried to give an account for the manner in which an unremarkable though talented Oxford professor was able to produce *The Lord of the Rings,* a story of such singular, unique beauty. However, their explanations usually describe only the "how," such as his brilliant philology and his breadth of medieval erudition. Admirers describe how he tended the magnificent tree of Middle-earth but fail to account for the seed and ground it grew in. Our Orthodox Tradition shows that nothing happens in a spiritual vacuum. The seed of Beauty is sown in ground that has been tilled by the cross of someone's self-emptying sacrifice.

Right before World War I, the young Tolkien was a member of a literary book club with whom he was very close. They all worked creatively together and kept in touch during the war. One member, Geoffrey Smith, stood out to Tolkien as a man of particular genius. His soul was cultivated; he had a gift to give the world that touched Tolkien. A few months before he was killed, Tolkien received this letter from him:

My chief consolation is that if I am scuppered tonight there will still be left a member [of our school group] to voice what I dreamed and what we all agreed upon. For the death of one of its members cannot, I am determined, dissolve [the group]. Death can make us loathsome and helpless as individuals, but it cannot put an end to the immortal four! May God bless you my dear John Ronald and may you say things I have tried to say long after I am not there to say them if such be my lot.[25]

The Lord, in His inscrutable wisdom, harvested this noble man's soul no doubt when it was at its ripest. However, I strongly believe that Smith's blessing, just before his entry into No Man's Land and his ultimate sacrifice, moved heaven to bestow upon Tolkien a special creative grace. God is never in debt, and the good dreams of those whose lives He allows to be cut short are never lost. The "immortal four" are beyond the veil now, but perhaps their shadows fall from the heights in the form of Frodo, Sam, Merry, and Pippin.

Moreover, on a different front of the same war, in the year before G. B. Smith died, another man was also offering himself to God in a total kenosis. In 1915, the armies of Russia were on the brink of defeat. Against the advice of all the officials who believed the war already lost and that association with the army was political suicide, Tsar Nicholas II took personal command of the army in a show of leadership that had not occurred since the days of Peter the Great. He said, "I will perish, but I will save Russia."[26]

The presence of the tsar in command had a remarkable effect on the war effort. His coming "strengthened the morale of the troops and their heroism reached its peak. Telegrams were flying to the front: 'The emperor is with us! Not a step back!'"[27]

In spite of a brilliant counteroffensive that forced the central powers to divert major forces from continental Europe, the tsar had been correct that the cost of victory would be his own death. A

---

25 John Garth, *Tolkien and the Great War: The Threshold of Middle-earth* (Houghton Mifflin Harcourt, 2013), 118.

26 St. John the Forerunner Monastery (authors), trans. Reverend George Lardas, *The Romanov Royal Martyrs: What Silence Could Not Conceal* (Mesa Potamos Publications, 2019), 193.

27 *The Romanov Royal Martyrs*, 193.

state of treasonous revolution was fomented in Moscow during his absence. German intelligence began a systemic campaign of espionage, slander, and political sabotage against the authority of the Romanovs in the great cities of Russia.[28] While Tsar Nicholas had been expending all his strength to save his country, the definitive groundwork for his usurpation had been laid by his own people in his absence. He was belittled, insulted, and slandered.

It is this Job-like suffering that confronts the reader of *The Romanov Royal Martyrs*. My pain in reading the account of the humiliation, exile, and murder of the tsar's whole family was intensified by understanding that this man truly did his best. He honored God and fought as hard as he could but still lost. His was the story of Job, a patriarch whose feast fell on the tsar's birthday, but where was the resurrection? A latent, primal dread surfaced: namely, that everything I love can be taken in a moment despite my best efforts. God did not explain himself to Job. I felt a taste of the fear that Job references when he said, "For the thing I greatly feared has come upon me, / And what I dreaded has happened to me" (Job 3:25).

And so I tore through the skete's archives, looking for accounts of Romanov miracles after their martyrdom. I wanted to know that there was life after such a horrible death. If God could lift Job and the Romanovs out of the grave, He could do the same for me. Then I too might have the courage to offer everything. I dug up all the issues of *The Orthodox Word* in the skete library concerning the Romanovs and read the miraculous accounts in them. During this search I found the akathist that had been translated by Fr. Seraphim Rose. My ultimate hope for consolation lay in making contact with the saints myself. It was this akathist I took with me to

---

28   *The Romanov Royal Martyrs*, 207.

Monk's Lagoon, saving it for the last of the three chapels. I prayed it by candlelight after dinner; it ends with these words:

> The Lord, testing thee like Job the Much-suffering, allowed there to come upon thee revilement, bitter sorrows, treason, betrayal, the estrangement of those close to thee, and the abdication of thine earthly kingdom amidst torment of soul. Having endured all this for the sake of the good of Russia as her faithful son, and having received a martyric death as a true servant of Christ, thou hast attained to the Heavenly Kingdom.[29]

I walked back to the cabin. I had not done the dishes and neglected to leave the holy water on the stove for washing, so it took me a long while to clear the pot and plate. By the time I finished, I was no longer thinking of the Romanovs but exploring the cabin a bit before I turned in. I noticed a white, unlabeled box on the shelf and opened it. Inside were small ziplock packets of dirt. By candlelight and the light of a lamp I began reading, "From the grave of Elder Leonid." Another read, "From the Grave of Grand Duchess Elizabeth and Nun Barbara." My heart began to beat faster. This was dirt from the grave of the sister-in-law of the tsar, a great saint, beloved in all North America.

Then I found a long splinter wrapped in white paper. For some time I could not make out the faded handwriting. At last I read, "Piece of Four Brothers Mine, Romanov Royal Martyrs." The distinctive fear in the presence of holiness gripped me then. My heart racing, I remembered from the book that initially the Communists

---

29 *The Royal Passion-bearers of Russia: Their Life and Service* (Herman of Alaska Brotherhood, 2014), 48.

had tried to hide the bodies of the Romanovs by throwing them down a mine shaft of the defunct Four Brothers Mine. The packets held relics left in this cabin by a pious pilgrim who had journeyed to Russia and visited these sites. It must have been decades ago, because churches have been built over these places, and such treasures can no longer be removed.

I prayed and venerated the dirt and wood. I felt that finding this treasure after the akathist to the tsar was the Romanovs' way of telling me that they were all right, that the Lord had not abandoned them but raised them up indeed as mighty, authentic saints of the Church. I could not leave the relics there but put them in a zipped, waterproof breast pocket of my jacket and carried them back to the skete. When I finally made it up the hill, I found Fr. Andrew by the parked four-wheeler. He blessed me, and I poured out my tale. He had not known about the white box and told me that this was indeed a special blessing from the Romanovs. He gifted me the relics, which I venerate daily still.

One last surprise was waiting for me. The mail run from Ouzinkie had brought a package full of pistachios from a friend, as well as a copy of the icon of the Grand Duchess Elizabeth that I had asked for months ago—the same grand duchess who wrote the following to her sister the tsaritsa in 1916:

> If we look deep into the life of every human, we discover that it is full of miracles. You will say, "Of terror and death, as well." Yes, that also. But we do not clearly see why the blood of these victims must flow. There, in the heavens, they understand everything and, no doubt, have found calm and True Homeland—a heavenly homeland. . . . Think of a storm; what sublime, frightening impressions. Some are so frightened,

others hide themselves, some perish, and others sense in all this the might of the Lord. Isn't that a picture of our times?[30]

She refers to the divine mystery of how suffering fits into God's plan. No one can give a full account of suffering, and God chastises the friends of Job for trying. Yet, there is a tradition in the Orthodox Church that in the whirlwind from which God spoke to Job, God revealed to Job the image of Himself on the Cross. So the answer to suffering is not an explanation but a theophany of God's co-suffering with us in the midst of our darkest moments—even a place so dark as the inner room where the Romanovs and their attendants were martyred.

The chapter recounting the event is unspeakably horrible. To have caught a glimpse of the beauty of their lives through the letters, photographs, and stories in the book, only to read about their graphic murder, is more than tragic. It's unacceptable, just as the death by shrapnel of Tolkien's friend, the sensitive young poet, Geoffrey Smith, is unacceptable. The absences of their lives are gaping wounds in the fabric of the whole cosmos. Yet all horror and tragedy are caught in the wingspan of the Lord's Cross. On Golgotha, He descended into each of those intolerable deaths. As St. Paul says, if we die in his death we will also rise with him (2 Tim. 2:11). Tolkien believed that stories could grant us a glimpse of that final victory. *The Lord of the Rings* is not an allegory, nor does the narrative map perfectly onto the life of Tsar Nicholas II and his family, but when Tolkien writes of glory with such power, I believe we get a glimpse of the glory that belongs to the saints. This is how he describes King Théoden riding to his final battle:

---

30 Liubov' Miller, *Grand Duchess Elizabeth of Russia: New Martyr of the Communist Yoke* (Nikodemos Orthodox Publication Society, 2009), 200–201.

Suddenly the king cried to Snowmane and the horse sprang away. Behind him his banner blew in the wind, white horse upon a field of green, but he outpaced it. ... His golden shield was uncovered, and lo! it shone like an image of the Sun, and the grass flamed into green about the white feet of his steed. For morning came, morning and a wind from the sea; the darkness was removed and the hosts of Mordor wailed, and terror took them, and they fled, and died, and the hooves of wrath rode over them.[31]

I received more glimpses of this resurrection from the relics I found in the white box in the skid cabin at Monk's Lagoon. The tsar was telling me that he's alive in Christ. My discovery of the relics was an assurance that Christ's Resurrection is strong enough even to turn that precious family's murder into glory. It was a sign that Christ does not abandon his people. The Romanovs are still with us, and if we follow their pattern of dying in Christ, we will get to be with them. We can say with the Russian soldiers on the front, "Not another step back! The emperor is with us!"

---

31   J. R. R. Tolkien, *The Lord of the Rings: Collector's Edition* (Houghton Mifflin, 1987), 112–113.

12

ℭWO RACES AGAINST THE SUN

ONE SUNDAY A BROTHER RECEIVED permission to go out on a hike to Monk's Lagoon by himself. Hiking from the skete to the holy sites where St. Herman lived takes anywhere from an hour and a half to three hours. So, six hours later at Vespers and afterward at trapeza, we were not overly concerned that he had not returned, though we all noted his empty place. The sun at last began to set, the dishes were done quietly, and everyone retired to their cells—but no one slept. We waited and prayed. At last, we heard Fr. Andrew's familiar tread going up the stairs to the second floor. Though I wanted his feet to stop outside my door, I knew they would not. I was not the best man for the mission. This quest belonged to my beloved friend Herman.

From the Tower I heard Fr. Andrew ask if Herman was willing to go back along the trail after the lost sheep. "Let's see if you can find him before we call the Coast Guard."

The fastest brother, a former wildland firefighter and a runner— there was no better man for the job. I longed to join him, but I knew that I would only encumber him. As I waited, prayed, and worried, I could vividly picture Herman moving through the Alaskan dusk. I knew he was striding, devouring the distance with huge steps. He would not be running, but striding as he raced to find the brother before the last of the sunlight was extinguished.

That wondrous novel *A Wrinkle in Time* is so named because the father of the protagonist has found a way to "wrinkle" space-time. The illustration given by the author, Madeleine L'Engle, is of an ant about to traverse a section of one of the characters' skirts. When the ends of a section are folded and brought together, the ant can step easily across.

Some men do this with their strides. Their purpose is so aligned with the purpose of space-time that it wrinkles to accommodate them. Perhaps this musing is just a poetic description of Herman moving fast, but I believe it is possible.

By now night had fallen. As the story was told afterward, the lost brother—who was new to Holy Orthodoxy—had been praying to be transported back to the skete miraculously. Then, tripping blindly through the brush, he saw a light coming toward him, shouting, "Jeremiah!"

"Who's there?"

"It's Herman!"

There was palpable relief in the skete when the brother returned. His plate was uncovered, and he sat down to it. The men of God all looked in on him to assure themselves he was well. I told him the next day that God had answered his prayer, just without teleportation. I had not yet thought of *A Wrinkle in Time*. The second race against the waning light occurred during a sunset later that year.

It seems that this liminal time is a time for accidents. The Alaskan sun is indeed slow in setting, which makes what Dr. Martin Shaw calls "the hour between dog and wolf" a long hour.

I will never forget the winter call from St. Nilus Skete that one of the nuns had fallen. The Coast Guard was summoned, and Fr. Andrew went over to support the operation in the *Archangel*. As providence would have it, the tide was out, giving the chopper the only possible landing site on the Fifty-Five-Acre Planet: the beach. I watched it from our island as it seemed to descend directly into the trees below.

The mother superior could not accompany the sister on the helicopter. So Fr. Andrew made a quick decision. He looked at the remains of the day and said to the mother superior, "We can make it, but we have to go now."

The *Archangel* has no lights of any kind on it. Like the silver moon, it reflects only whatever light is given by the sun. So, the vessel does not ever travel at night. Now Fr. Andrew was going to race the sun to Kodiak. Ordinarily, he slows if the waves are choppy; he surfs on them. Not so that night; I knew he cut straight through. On land Brother Herman had to wrinkle space to move faster, but the Gulf of Alaska is already fretted with the myriad wrinkles we call waves. So in a sense, to traverse this medium with haste, the hegumen had to maintain a linear, straight path. It was not a comfortable crossing. The *Archangel* put her shoulder down and charged straight through, bisecting the waves with her prow and drenching her passengers with the protesting spray.

I am still amazed at how Fr. Andrew makes these decisions. How did he know to send Herman before calling the Coast Guard? How could he have the confidence to navigate the Kodiak coastline, with its many shoals and sharp rocks, in the dying light?

So the spiritual mother of the nuns and the spiritual father of the monks tore after the chopper, following by sea. Each had their best headlamps strapped to their foreheads. A surreal sight greeted them in the Kodiak dock.

Unbeknownst to them, it was the evening of the Kodiak Christmas light boat parade. Before them stretched a line of dazzlingly lit boats of every size, each draped with yuletide LED colors, all their running lights ablaze. Then, emerging blinking from the night, black robes and waterproof bibs drenched by saltwater, the monastics crossed into this halo of light. Did they reach up and turn off their headlamps? Or did they materialize from the gloom as some aquatic miners from their deep-water caverns to pay homage to the Christ child?

This image of the two of them entering the circle of those bright lights stands out starkly in my imagination as an image of their angelic vocation. With their legendary hospitality, disarming calm, and unassuming manner, they set at ease new acquaintances who have not encountered monastics before. I have grown up around monastics, so the holy strangeness of their vocation does not strike me often. However, that night it was impossible to ignore. Shrouded in their dark robes, in the obscurity of the far edge of civilization, they are hidden from the world to reveal their innermost depths to God for healing. In the wilds of the forest, they try to tame their passions. They spend their lives thus, only returning to civilization at need. Even then, their otherworldly appearance reminds us that the Greek word for saint is *agios*, "not of this earth." That night they made it to the hospital and supported the nun, who with great courage and determination made a full recovery. And when she was ready, she returned by boat to the island she had left by helicopter to continue sailing through dark waters to the harbor of Christ.

Whether the distance is crossed by wrinkling the land or by cutting a straight line across the cowlicked sea, the monastics are always traveling into the darkness to find the light of a Person. When the goal is Christ, who lives inside the lost brother or injured sister, time and space are traversed in a mystical way. Unknowing of the "facts" of clock time or distance, some of the fathers have lived on Spruce Island for over twenty-five years. If it is impossible to imagine that length of time spent in the struggle, it is more impossible to imagine the Person of the Lord who is even now drawing them through time and space to Himself. He must be so passing Beautiful that all the vicissitudes of the diurnal and nocturnal hours, all the wrinkles of space, are no obstacle to the one who chases Him.

13

THE RUINOUS STUFF OF BEAUTY

WHEN THE WAVES ARE ALL frothing like popped champagne in the channel, there is only one way to the post office: the Ouzinkie road. Ouzinkie, the only other inhabited part of the island, is a tiny village of a little over a hundred souls. It has a large dock and an airstrip, remnants from when it was a larger fishing town, but many of its people have moved to Kodiak. Near the dock, flying the stars and stripes, is the post office.

The ATV can't make the trip, so in winter when the wind blew through the channel, making the trip impossible for the *Archangel* as well, it was the great privilege of myself and Herman to traverse the frozen expanse with chains on our boots and forty-liter waterproof bags strapped on our backs. A few times we brought a homemade metal rig on which we could stack packages then bungee-cord them into place.

Down the hill we flew, through the abandoned neighborhood of Sunny Cove to the Ouzinkie road. In winter even the seasonal hunters are gone, and besides two neighbors who visit the skete for Liturgy, the borough is truly a ghost town. Most buildings are abandoned; they sag and molder like decomposing trees, which is essentially what they are made of. Once abandoned by their builders, the life goes out of them. The boards that were once trees offer shelter to no one and stand as forlorn monuments to the dreams and hopes of the people who built them.

On the way to the post office, we passed the turning to the house of a homesteader who had tried to live out here like Thoreau at Walden Pond. Only, despite his myriad books and hobbies, he was dreadfully lonely—though Fr. Andrew told me he had a knack for always showing up at the skete just when an extra pair of hands was needed. Eventually he sold his lot and his house to St. Michael's Skete. One of the main projects I worked on during my pilgrimage was deconstructing his house from the roof down to salvage every usable board.

The task really helped me understand the inextricable relationship between a man's psyche and his home. He was an inexperienced carpenter who built by following the maxim, "If you don't know where to nail, nail a lot." When I used my sledge to knock the rafter to the floor, at the end of each board I could see the rat's nest of half a dozen twisted nails to keep it in place. It seemed as if each nail had been driven in to fix his dreams in physical space, as if the house were an incarnation of his hopes. He had left much stuff behind, and I felt for him, especially when I saw the mass market paperback of *The Hobbit* and a VHS tape of season one of *Star Trek: The Next Generation* gathering damp.

It was a sad place that we unmade board by board. We crowbarred up the second floor methodically, starting with the plywood then the joists beneath, working backward toward the stairs as we were removing the very structure we were standing on. When all that had fastened the walls in place was removed, we simply pushed them over with our gloved hands. I imagined most of the houses we passed on our way through the borough had similar insides.

Even the road to Ouzinkie was falling apart. Allegedly, the man responsible for building this road saved much of the grant money by building it with a group of adventurers from the lower forty-eight who paid him for the privilege of being Alaskan trailblazers. The team's lack of expertise is apparent in the absence of drains built into the logs lining the whole road. During the ubiquitous rains, the road becomes a 3.5-mile gutter, with the dirt washing out from beneath the grids of anti-erosion rubber mats that cover the surface.

Herman and I enjoyed our speed while it lasted. There is a special romance to using a road no one uses; every bend had not been seen since you had last seen it. Once again, the fathers had entrusted us with a mission: We were to bring back not just the mail for St. Michael's Skete but for St. Nilus Skete as well. To us were vouchsafed both sets of P.O. box keys. If the postmaster was absent, we would be able to gather all the precious mail. Our talk was even freer during those jaunts. The way there was quick, not so the way back.

When our sacks were laden with boxes, postcards, notes, and letters strapped to our backs, the return journey loomed before us. Once, around Christmastime, the load was especially heavy. Herman, ever the stronger man, wore a metal rig on his chest and piled his knapsack to the brim behind him. I staggered under my lighter load—even one mile downhill with that weight seemed absurd. I could not imagine carrying it all the way. Yet how could I lag behind a man of such honor? He bore the heavier burden so that I could continue. Not for the first time I was reminded that shame and honor are not on the same continuum. To be without honor is not to be shamed; it simply means that one has not yet encountered

an honorable person. But when we find him, we shift the weight of
our pack, tighten the straps, and totter after him so as not to lose
sight of his golden light. Not because we are ashamed to be left
behind, but for the love of his company.

As we left Ouzinkie that day, past the village dump to where
the gravel road met the washed-out rubber matting of the path, the
load was somehow bearable—as if there were a peculiar magic to
the packages and letters sent to the Alaskan monastics. As if there
were a lightness to the secret thoughts, prayers, wishes, and mes-
sages enclosed in the letters on our backs. Who does not wish to
be a little like Father Christmas, traipsing through the snow with a
delivery someone is sure to be grateful for? The items were imbued
with the unknown; perhaps it was a book that the mother superior
of the nuns had been so looking forward to reading. Maybe there
was a letter, long awaited by one of the brethren.

Of course, if there was something addressed to me, that was best
of all. I tried not to look at the letters as I stuffed them into a Zip-
loc bag for further moisture protection, but I thrilled when I saw
my name written on an envelope. I hadn't realized how much I was
engaged in affirming my own existence to myself until the moment
I saw my name written in someone else's hand. Then I briefly
relaxed the effort of assuring myself that I am really here. Someone else had acknowledged my existence in writing. Some corre-
spondents put ornate loops on the "A," others wrote "Mr.," and some
had doodles. There was a delicious interlude of just letting them sit,
pregnant on my desk in the Tower. After chapel and dinner, when
all chores were done and goodnights were said, I could climb the
steps and be alone with the mail. I ordered them by the criterion of
"one I am least excited about" to "the best for last." Then I tore into
them. Often I was surprised that my ordering did not play out in
the way I expected.

When opening a new letter from a friend, I liked to have all our previous correspondence within reach. The comparison between the letters told me almost as much as their contents. I felt like a detective getting to the bottom of another person's heart. There were cryptic patterns, such as how long someone spent decrying the state of her penmanship or rejoicing that she had an opportunity to write a letter. Often, I could tell the moment in the missive when she acclimated to the medium and began to compose with real substance. Sometimes, she would repeat news shared in a previous letter, and other times she went back and spoke to me through the margins.

It struck me that margins were a way of going back in time. Even by the end of the letter, my correspondent was a different person than the one speaking in the margin. So I paid rapt attention, even to grammatical edits. Corrections were the latest layer of psychic strata. Each letter formed another layer until the whole correspondence was like a spiritual fingerprint of the person. If the houses in the borough were a physical reflection of the builder's inner world, then the letters too might be a linguistic mirror reflecting their psyche.

About six months into my pilgrimage, I happened across this quote on the deceptive nature of correspondence from one of Franz Kafka's letters in which he explains why he abhors writing them:

The easy possibility of letter writing must—seen merely theoretically—have brought into the world a terrible disintegration of souls. It is, in fact, an intercourse with ghosts, and not only with the ghost of the recipient but also with one's own ghost, which develops between the lines of the letter one is writing and even more so in a series of letters where one letter corroborates the other and can refer to it as a witness.

How on earth did anyone get the idea that people can com-
municate with one another by letter! Of a distant person one
can think, and of a person who is near one can catch hold—all
else goes beyond human strength.[32]

According to Kafka, the cipher that I so enjoyed was not the key
to a true person, but to the ghost of a person—an ideal, created of
words and paper, acting as an intermediary across distances. So,
the correspondence, especially as I began to keep copies of my own
responses, was creating a dialogue between ghostly impressions.
On Spruce Island I was caught in the tension between the living
home of the skete and the dead houses in the borough. Likewise
I was caught between the tension of embodied interactions with
the fathers and the disembodied ideal that I presented to people
through my letters. Much as I loved missives, they were only point-
ers to the incarnated reality of the other. This embodied experience
of the Real is mediated by the five senses, which each interact with
a different aspect of the object or person encountered. One thing
I have noticed repeatedly in the stories I love is that if something
is a lie, at least one of the senses revolts. The laden banquet table
looks sumptuous, but the air in the room feels damp and oppres-
sive. The maiden seems fair, but her laugh is the grate of a hag.
When Gandalf is lost in Moria, he follows his nose, choosing the
path that smells less foul. One dose of reality is enough to dissipate
the imaginary confusion or navigate the dark labyrinth where the
line between the real and imagined is blurred.

Consider taste, for example. When did you last drink a glass of
the black currant wine of St. Michael's Skete in a dream? Never.

---

32 Quoted in Harold Bloom, *The Western Canon: The Books and School of the
Ages* (Harcourt Brace & Company, 1994), 420.

Perhaps you never had such an ambrosial drink even waking. That wine is more than memory, more than thought or signifier; it is a bottle of the island, merry as a clap on the back. A dream would not survive such a wonderful taste. The flavor would burn the dream away into waking through sheer deliciousness. Likewise our auditory sense, through which we hear melodies so beautiful that they are ruinous to imaginary fantasies. Never will I forget when a neighbor, Lasalle, opened his guitar case after Liturgy and trapeza. I was doing dishes with Herman, and we heard his voice from the second story. He had "the voice," the one the show is always looking for but can't find because he is in Alaska hunting with his dad. It wasn't just a fine voice, one that could be molded into an exceptional performer; this man was a bard. He slew us. The resonance of his voice would vibrate to pieces any ghost within earshot. In particular, he sang a Jerry Lee Lewis song, "She Even Woke Me Up to Say Goodbye," in which an abandoned man with Hosea-like fidelity continues to defend his love to God and man.

It was the ruinous stuff of beauty. His song was so poignant that it won through all the airy fantasies around me to pierce my heart through my ears. His performance was altogether more physically immediate than any of the recorded songs I listened to—an unrepeatable event. Even should he sing the same song again, it would be an altogether new theophany. A repeatable recording would sound tinny, pale, and insubstantial against his song, which was an embodied expression of his ever-dynamic person.

Oh, Lasalle, return to us once more. Long have I looked for your coming from the Tower. I asked after you even since I left Spruce, but you had not returned. Do not tarry until the end of days, when you are called to the stage to play the end credits of the world.

If Lasalle is beauty through hearing, Herman is the same through touch. His farewell embrace is a fierce hug. It's a promise that my back is within the circle of his protection, that he is look-ing over my shoulder, and that he'll face down whatever is lurking there. If we found ourselves trapped in a dream, we would fight our way free.

Thus the goodness of Creation is affirmed as specific instances in the world of the senses become iconographic, and illusion is destroyed. Beauty cannot help itself; everything bursts into flame in its presence, and the only completely noncombustible thing is the human heart. Because Beauty is personal, He reveals Himself through specific theophanies in each person's life. Consider the lit-any against the darkness which Julie Andrews sings in *The Sound of Music*. Her favorite things include cream-colored ponies, schnitzel with noodles, and "silver-white winters which melt into springs."[33] This is not nostalgic; it's iconographic. She is not being consoled by sentimental memory but experiencing anew the same grace that came through those experiences. It was one of her favorite things, "brown paper packages tied up with string," that Herman and I were carrying on our backs to the skete.

Thus laden we at last left the washed-out trail and reentered Sunny Cove borough. If ever there were a space that is haunted, it would be the buildings on these abandoned properties. They were homemade houses, some of plywood, others of more substantial lumber, all moldering away. There was the house of a homeschool family who came for a few seasons to live in a holy wild place. Hunt-ing houses, houses of hippies, houses of eccentric millionaires. What they have in common is that they are all abandoned, lifeless, and full of trash. There is a deep trench that served as some kind of communal dump; it is filled with cans and all manner of debris. There are gutted four-by-fours and rusty canoes and rotted dories.

---

33 *The Sound of Music*, directed by Robert Wise (20th Century Fox, 1965).

Yet the resurrection of these places has already begun in the lot of the house we disassembled. Where it once stood is one of the secret sources of dirt for the monks' garden. The punky boards were burned, the sound but misshapen boards fortified a garden terrace, and the best of this salvaged lumber we carried in a previous chapter for the building of a new monastic cell. I hope the previous owner was consoled by the physical remains of his dream being integrated into the life of the community once more.

Puffing and covered in sweat, we began our final ascent up the hill. The terraced vegetable garden looked like the stairs of a giant leading to the red ochre walls of the skete, perched on the highest point in the borough, looking out to the sea from its many-sized windows.

The three little pigs built houses of straw, sticks, and brick. The skete was a stick house, better than straw, but when the wolf blew through the trees, I could feel the whole building creak and sway like the hull of an old galleon. Still, the wolf never blew it down. The floorboards were nailed straight onto the ceiling joists; the bones of the building are built with care but not expertise. It is a peculiar kind of ship, an ark built by inexperienced Noahs. Every snore, sneeze, or sob can be heard through the cracks. When Fr. Andrew unexpectedly needed to go out on the skiff, I would materialize to serve as a deckhand, since I had heard the conversation.

It was a rectangular rather than hexagonal beehive. The bees dispersed to chapel and work, then returned to their fragile, honey-colored cells. The building seems so fragile to me now, so insubstantial. Even on Kodiak only one building remains from the time of St. Herman, because wood does not last more than a few decades here.

Earlier I described how one beautiful thing can burn away a bad dream. However, on Spruce Island, the beautiful dominates, and it burns away ugly houses with a million tongues of mossy green flame. The forest swallows them. The island is a healthy, well-ordered microcosm. What it expels are the germs that would contaminate it. What it does not expel it incorporates as part of its body. That is why the buildings of the skete, especially the new chapel, have come to look as if they grew from the island itself. Since much of the lumber for it was milled from nearby trees, it literally did grow from the island. But the true reason it endures is the Liturgy burning but not consuming it in its heart. To write this from outside the island is painful. I did not last there either. I could not stay, much as Jerry Lee's lady could not. I know the fathers pray for me, and a very diluted, poetic abstraction of that prayer might be called, "He Even Wrote a Book to Say Goodbye."

RACE YOU TO THE TOP

I took every possible opportunity to ride in the *Archangel* and serve as a deckhand to Fr. Andrew. He had at last succeeded in teaching me a sailor's knot when he demonstrated a sheepshank on a shoelace: "Rabbit jumps out of the hole, goes round the tree, and jumps back in the hole."

Every time I tied us off, I whispered this archetypical story like an incantation with each loop. It held fast like any true story on a shoelace, on a running line, in my heart. After I pulled her out to the buoy, Fr. Andrew and I would admire that view of Sunny Cove. We never tired of seeing the *Archangel* at rest.

I did not speak, letting the moment last as long as it possibly could, though each of those blessed silences seem to live outside of time. Sometimes I imagine that I have not left—that I'm really there right now on the beach and that the rest of my life is a postscript to that view.

At last Father would turn with a smile and say, "Race you to the top." And I would take off like a shot! No longer did I need him to await me at each turning of the road as I had on the day of my arrival. I knew every bend of that path now; I knew the shortcuts and the best fords across the creek. My head start always consisted of him lashing the boxes and supplies to the four-wheeler with bungee cords. But soon, always too soon, I would hear the motor growling behind me ever louder like some hound of heaven. My heart pounded with exhilaration and effort as I willed myself higher to reach the skete before he did. I contrived to bend the scenery with my strides, to tilt the world around me so I could somehow fall upward and reach the summit before he did.

He beat me every time.

His four-wheeler was no unfair advantage. He rode it as an extension of his own body, capturing the machine into the joyous upsurge of his personhood. I could never be disappointed when I saw him pass by.

But let him be warned. He has set me on the trail, and I continue to race.

We hope you have enjoyed and benefited from this book. Your financial support makes it possible to continue our nonprofit ministry both in print and online. Because the proceeds from our book sales only partially cover the costs of operating **Ancient Faith Publishing** and **Ancient Faith Radio**, we greatly appreciate the generosity of our readers and listeners. Donations are tax deductible and can be made at **www.ancientfaith.com.**

To view our other publications, please visit our website:
store.ancientfaith.com

ANCIENT FAITH
RADIO

Bringing you Orthodox Christian music, readings, prayers, teaching, and podcasts 24 hours a day since 2004 at
www.ancientfaith.com

www.ingramcontent.com/pod-product-compliance
Lightning Source LLC
Chambersburg PA
CBHW020418150626
46554CB00014B/1930